$15.00

FLAN ON' COOKBOOK

Food for RVers, Campers, Bikers, Hikers, Hobos and Travelers

By Tim Murphy

Copyright 2017
Shamrock Arrow Media

For information on the entire series of "Flannel John's Cookbooks" visit www.flanneljohn.com

FLANNEL JOHN'S ON THE ROAD COOKBOOK

Food for RVers, Campers, Bikers, Hikers, Hobos and Travelers

TABLE OF CONTENTS

SANDWICHES	**Page 11**
After Thanksgiving Turkey Sandwich	Page 13
Barbecue Beef Sandwich	Page 14
Bohemian Wraps 'N Cheese	Page 15
Crab Sandwich	Page 16
Cuban Sandwich	Page 17
Dagwood Sandwich	Page 18
Danish Tuna Fish Sandwich	Page 19
Elk Meatloaf Sandwich	Page 20
Grilled Cheese & Cranberry	Page 21
Grilled Cheese & Pear Sandwich	Page 22
Grilled Three-Cheese Sandwich	Page 23
Italian Grinder	Page 24
King Elvis Sandwich	Page 25
Loose Meat Sandwich	Page 26

Mushroom Sandwich _____ Page 27
Pork Overload Sandwich _____ Page 28
Reuben Sliders _____ Page 29
Salami Wraps _____ Page 30
Sloppy Buck BBQ Sandwich _____ Page 31
Spicy BBQ Pork Sandwich _____ Page 32
Spritely Gobble Sandwich _____ Page 33
Turkey Sourdough Sandwich _____ Page 34
Two Rivers Meatloaf Sandwich _____ Page 35
Walking Taco _____ Page 36

COOKING WITH FIRE _____ **Page 39**
Apple Dumplings _____ Page 41
Baby Carrots _____ Page 42
Barbecue Pork Burger _____ Page 43
Beef Barbecue Sandwiches _____ Page 44
Beef Jerky Chili _____ Page 45
Beer Can Chicken _____ Page 46
BLT Burger _____ Page 47
Brats On a Stick _____ Page 48
Breakfast Hash _____ Page 49
Cabin Potatoes _____ Page 50
Cajun Shrimp _____ Page 51
Campers Mix _____ Page 52
Campfire Burgers _____ Page 53
Campfire Coffee _____ Page 54
Campfire Potatoes _____ Page 55
Campfire Split _____ Page 56
Caribbean Turkey Burger _____ Page 57

Cast Iron Cookies	Page 58
Catfish Cakes	Page 59
Catfish Stew	Page 60
Cherry Almond Pork Chops	Page 61
Chicago-Style Hot Dogs	Page 62
Clam Fritters	Page 63
Classic Burger	Page 64
Collard Greens	Page 65
Crawfish Stew	Page 66
Curses, Foiled Again Fish	Page 67
Deer Camp Chili	Page 68
Dutch Oven Camp Breakfast	Page 69
Dutch Oven Corn Bread	Page 70
Flounder Dinner	Page 71
Fruit Soup	Page 72
Garlic Shrimp	Page 73
Gator Stew	Page 74
Grilled Duck	Page 75
Grilled King Salmon	Page 76
Grilled Sirloin	Page 77
Huevos Rancheros	Page 78
Jalapeno Poppers	Page 79
Honey-Lime Grilled Chicken	Page 80
Island Steak	Page 81
Lamb Burger	Page 82
Lemon Herb Chicken	Page 83
Meat Kabobs	Page 84
Mushrooms & Scallops	Page 85
Mustard Dill Salmon	Page 86

New Mexico Chicken _____ Page 87
Oatmeal with Apples _____ Page 88
Polish Sausage in Beer _____ Page 89
Portobello Mushrooms _____ Page 90
Quesadilla _____ Page 91
Root Beer Chicken _____ Page 92
Salmon Steaks _____ Page 93
Seafood Pot _____ Page 94
Shore Lunch Trout _____ Page 95
Skillet Beans _____ Page 96
Smelt on the Coals _____ Page 97
S'mores Popcorn _____ Page 98
Snow Peas _____ Page 99
Squirrel Stew _____ Page 100
Summer Burger _____ Page 101
Turkey Chili Burger _____ Page 102
Venison & Mushrooms _____ Page 103
Vegetable Soup _____ Page 104
Venison In the Pot _____ Page 105

SLOW COOKER RECIPES _____ **Page 107**
All-Day Stew _____ Page 109
Applesauce _____ Page 110
Bacon Cheese Dip _____ Page 111
Baked Chicken _____ Page 112
Baked Oatmeal _____ Page 113
Banana Bread _____ Page 114
Barbecued Chicken _____ Page 115
Barbecued Game Steak _____ Page 116

Barbecued Ham	Page 117
Barbecued Hot Dogs	Page 118
Barbecued Riblets	Page 119
Beef & Green Beans	Page 120
Beef Barbecue	Page 121
Beef Roast	Page 122
Beef Stew	Page 123
Beef Stroganoff	Page 124
Beer Brats	Page 125
Big Chunk 'O Beef	Page 126
Big Game Chicken Wings	Page 127
Bologna & Sauerkraut	Page 128
Brunswick Stew	Page 129
Catfish Stew	Page 130
Chicken & Mushrooms	Page 131
Chicken Gumbo	Page 132
Chicken Potato Casserole	Page 133
Chicken Reuben Pot	Page 134
Chili with Beans	Page 135
Chili Cheese Dip	Page 136
Chili Nuts	Page 137
Clam Chowder	Page 138
Cola Beef	Page 139
Cola Chicken	Page 140
Colcannon	Page 141
Corned Beef	Page 142
Crab Soup	Page 143
Cranberry Chicken	Page 144
Creamy Red Potatoes	Page 145

Crock Pot Pizza	Page 146
Dutch Oven Camp Breakfast	Page 147
Elk & Kraut	Page 148
Georgia Ribs	Page 149
Glazed Carrots	Page 150
Gourmet Tomato Soup	Page 151
Grandma's Minestrone	Page 152
Greek Chicken	Page 153
Hawaiian Ribs	Page 154
Hambone Soup	Page 155
Homemade Baked Beans	Page 156
Hunter's Chicken	Page 157
Italian Chicken	Page 158
Italian Pork Chops	Page 159
Jerky Chili	Page 160
Kraut & Kielbasa	Page 161
Lamb with Herbs	Page 162
Lazy Chops	Page 163
Low & Slow Chili	Page 164
Logging Camp Stew	Page 165
Meatloaf	Page 166
Meatloaf II	Page 167
Orchard Soup	Page 168
Oyster Stew	Page 169
Pepper Chicken	Page 170
Pizza Rice	Page 171
Pork Chops & Gravy	Page 172
Pork Roast	Page 173
Pot Roast	Page 174

Refried Bean Dip_____Page 175
Rice Pudding_____Page 176
Seafood Pot_____Page 177
Simple Chicken_____Page 178
Sloppy Chicken_____Page 179
Slow Burn Beans_____Page 180
Slow Poke Pork_____Page 181
Snow Day Stew_____Page 182
South of the Border Beans_____Page 183
Spiced Apple Cider_____Page 184
Spicy Pork Chops_____Page 185
Teriyaki Chicken_____Page 186
Tropical Chicken_____Page 187
Tuna Salad Casserole_____Page 188
Turkey Breast Bake_____Page 189
Turkey Chili_____Page 190
Turkey Stew_____Page 191
Vegetable Beef Soup_____Page 192
Venison Chili_____Page 193
Whole Wheat & Cornmeal Bread_____Page 194
Witches Cauldron Stew_____Page 195
Worth-The-Wait Beef Stew_____Page 196

FORAGED FOOD_____Page 199
Acorn Cakes_____Page 201
Beech Leaves_____Page 202
Berry Soup_____Page 203
Birch Leaf Salad_____Page 204
Blackberry Leaf Tea_____Page 205

Blue Camas Bulbs	Page 206
Buttered Nettles	Page 207
Cattail Pollen Cakes	Page 208
Chaparral Tea	Page 209
Chickweed Salad	Page 210
Chippewa Bannock	Page 211
Clams & Seaweed	Page 212
Creamed Chickweed	Page 213
Dandelion Salad	Page 214
Dry Roasted Grasshoppers	Page 215
Elderberry Tea	Page 216
Fiddlehead Stew	Page 217
Fireweed & Clover Honey	Page 218
Fish & Cattails	Page 219
Fried Morel Mushrooms	Page 220
Hazelnut Soup	Page 221
Hickory Milk	Page 222
Homesteader's Salad	Page 223
Lamb's Quarter Greens	Page 224
Lemon Balm Sun Tea	Page 225
Maple Tree Seeds	Page 226
Milkweed Soup	Page 227
Pine Syrup	Page 228
Pinon Cakes	Page 229
Red Clover Biscuits	Page 230
Rice, Nuts & Berries	Page 231
Sassafras Cherry Tea	Page 232
Sautéed Fiddleheads	Page 233
Silverweed (Wild Sweet Potato)	Page 234

Spicewood Tea_____Page 235
Steamed Clams_____Page 236
Steamed Milkweed Pods_____Page 237
Sunflower Seed Cakes_____Page 238
Sunflower Seed Soup_____Page 239
Watercress Salad_____Page 240
White Cedar Tea_____Page 241
Wild Green Salad_____Page 242
Wild Lilac Tea_____Page 243
Wild Peppermint Tea_____Page 244
Wild Rice Bake_____Page 245
Wild Strawberry Vinegar_____Page 246
Willow Bud Salad_____Page 247

BREAKFAST – DAY STARTERS_____Page 249
Baked Oatmeal_____Page 251
Big Cheese Omelet_____Page 252
Blueberry & Wild Rice Breakfast_____Page 253
Breakfast Bacon Pie_____Page 254
Buttermilk Pancakes_____Page 255
Farmer's Breakfast_____Page 256
French Toast_____Page 257
Fresh Scrambled Eggs_____Page 258
Ham & Egg Scramble_____Page 259
Hash Brown Breakfast_____Page 260
Morning Health Shake_____Page 261
Omelet In a Bag_____Page 262
Seven-Pound Breakfast_____Page 263
Trail Breakfast Granola_____Page 264

Sandwiches

Hot and Cold

AFTER THANKSGIVING TURKEY SANDWICH

2 slices of rye bread, seedless if possible
4 slices of turkey
3 ounces of Brie cheese, thinly sliced
2 tablespoons of cranberry Sauce
1 teaspoon of oil

Heat the oil in a skillet or on a grill. Place the bread on a medium-hot skillet and layer 2 pieces of cheese on each bread slice. Let the cheese melt a little. Layer turkey on one slice of the rye bread and top with cranberry sauce. Bring the 2 slices together and continue to heat until golden brown, about 3 to 4 minutes per sides.

BARBECUE BEEF SANDWICHES

4 pounds of lean beef, cut into chunks
14 ounces of tomatoes, canned
2 medium onions, diced
1 quart of water
1 cup of ketchup
1 tablespoon of chili powder
½ cup of vinegar
½ cup of Worcestershire sauce
Salt and pepper to taste
Garlic powder to taste
Liquid smoke (optional)
Hamburger buns

Combine all ingredients in a Dutch oven or large soup pot. Simmer uncovered on low heat for 5 to 6 hours or until beef falls to shreds. The mixture should be thick. Spoon the beef mixture onto hoagie or crusty rolls.

BOHEMIAN WRAPS 'N CHEESE

Sun-dried tomato and basil wraps
Fresh spinach
Tomatoes, diced
Feta Cheese
Mozzarella cheese, shredded or sliced
Salt and pepper to taste

Spread sour cream over one side of the wrap. Add spinach, cheeses and seasoning to taste.

CRAB SANDWICH

½ pound of fresh crabmeat
1 cup of tomato soup
½ onion, grated
2 teaspoons of mayonnaise
½ pound of Cheddar cheese, grated
6 English muffins or bagels

Mix first five ingredients and spreads on muffin or bagel halves. Bake at 350 degrees for 12 minutes.

CUBAN SANDWICH

1 loaf of Cuban bread
1 pound of ham
   (sweet cured ham or bolo ham works best)
1 pound of Cuban pork (or roast pork)
½ pound of Swiss cheese
16 slices of dill pickle
Butter

His recipe makes 4 sandwiches. Heat a griddle or large fry pan to medium hot. Cut bread into 8-inch sections then slice these in half. Spread butter inside on both halves. Layer ingredients as follows: pickles, roast pork, ham and cheese. Spread a little butter on the hot griddle or fry pan and place the sandwich on the hot surface. Use a foil-wrapped brick to flatten the sandwich. Squeeze it down to half or a third or its original size. Grill the sandwiches for two to three minutes then flip them over to toast the other side. Once the cheese is melted and the bread is golden brown on both sides, the sandwiches are done.

DAGWOOD SANDWICH

6 dill pickle chips
4 slices of deli ham
4 slices of bologna
4 slices of salami
4 slices of deli turkey
3 slices of rye bread
3 slices of tomato
2 slices of American cheese
2 slices of Swiss cheese
2 leaves of iceberg lettuce
2 green olives stuffed with pimento
Mustard
Mayonnaise

Spread mustard on 2 slices of bread and mayonnaise on the third slice. Top one of the mustard slices with ham, American cheese, lettuce and bologna. Top the second mustard slice with salami, pickle chips, tomato slices, turkey, Swiss cheese and the third slice of rye mayonnaise side down. Stack this group on the first group. Skewer each olive with a toothpick and secure the sandwich. For your safety, remove toothpicks before eating.

DANISH TUNA SANDWICH

12 ounces of tuna fish
1 cup of cabbage, coarsely grated
1 cup of carrot, coarsely grated
1 tablespoon of ketchup
3 tablespoons of mayonnaise
1 tablespoon of lemon juice
½ teaspoon of salt
Pepper to taste

Drain and flake the tuna in a bowl. Mix tuna with carrots and cabbage. In a separate bowl mix ketchup, mayonnaise, lemon juice, salt and pepper together. Add both mixtures and toss. Serve on open-face buttered toast.

ELK MEATLOAF SANDWICH

2 pounds of ground elk
1 pound of ground beef
1 cup of water
1 package of dry onion soup mix
Hamburger buns

Combine all ingredients until well blended. Form into 2 loaves and bake uncovered in a loaf pan or baking dish at 350 degrees for 90 minutes. Let cool before slicing. Serve on hamburger buns with ketchup or hot sauce.

GRILLED CHEESE & CRANBERRY SANDWICH

Cheddar cheese, grated
Cranberries, fresh and coarsely chopped
2 slices of bread, thick or dense if possible
Butter
Dijon mustard or honey mustard, optional

Mix grated cheese and cranberries together. Spread butter on both sides of the slices. Spread the mixture on 1 slice of bread and choice of mustard on the other (optional). Close up the sandwich and grill on a medium-hot griddle or skillet. Sandwich is done when bread turns golden brown, about 4 minutes per side.

GRILLED CHEESE & PEAR SANDWICH

Sour Dough Bread
Butter or Margarine
Sliced Sharp Cheddar
Sliced Havarti
Mayonnaise
Creamy Horse Radish Sauce
French's French Fried Onions
Pear Jam or Preserves
(peach or apricot work too)

For each sandwich butter one side of each slice of bread. On the other, spread one with a mixture of mayonnaise and horseradish sauce and one with the pear jam. Then between the 2 slices, add a slice of each cheese and French fried onions. Close and fry in pan until golden brown and cheese has melted.

GRILLED THREE-CHEESE SANDWICH

3 ounces of softened cream cheese
¾ cup mayonnaise
1 cup shredded cheddar cheese
1 cup shredded mozzarella cheese
½ teaspoon garlic powder
Dash of seasoning salt
10 slices of Italian bread (½ inch thick)
2 tablespoons butter

In a bowl, mix cream cheese and mayonnaise until smooth. Stir in cheese, garlic powder and seasoning salt. Spread 5 slices of bread with cheese mixture and top with remaining bread. Butter outside of sandwich and toast in a large pan or skillet for about 4 minutes a side or until golden brown.

ITALIAN GRINDER

4 sub rolls (Italians bread, hoagie, etc.)
Hot capicola ham
Pepperoni, large-style slices
Genoa salami, sliced thin
Provolone cheese, sliced thin
Tomato, sliced thin
Shredded iceberg lettuce
Italian dressing (optional)

Toast your rolls with the inside of the bread facing up. Load up the bottom half of the bun with the three meats, topping them with cheese. Return to oven and cook until cheese starts to melt and gets a little bubbly. Once it reaches desired toastiness, remove from oven and top with lettuce, tomato and dressing.

KING ELVIS SANDWICH

8 hot dog buns split
Peanut Butter (smooth or chunky)
Butter or margarine
2 tablespoons of honey
4 sliced bananas
1 teaspoon of cinnamon (optional)

Toast and butter the hot dog buns. Stir together peanut butter, honey and cinnamon (optional) and spread on the interior of the buns. Top with a split banana half. Serves eight or one overweight musical icon.

LOOSE MEAT SANDWICH

3 pounds of ground beef
4 cups of beef broth
¼ cup of onion, diced fine
3 tablespoons of Worcestershire sauce
2 teaspoons of butter
1 teaspoon of salt
1 teaspoon of pepper
Hamburger buns

In a pan, cook crumbled ground beef and diced onion over medium-high heat. While cooking, keep stirring and break up the lumps. Cook until browned and no longer pink. Drain off the grease and add Worcestershire sauce, beef broth, salt, pepper and butter. Bring to a boil, then set heat on low and simmer uncovered for 35 to 45 minutes or until the liquid is almost gone. Remove from heat, cover, and let sit for 15 minutes. Scoop onto hamburger buns. Makes 10 to 12 sandwiches.

MUSHROOM SANDWICH

4 ounces of canned mushrooms, chopped
1 ounce of Parmesan cheese
1 ounce of Monterey Jack cheese, sliced
1 tablespoon of onion, minced
1 tablespoon of mustard
¼ teaspoon of thyme
2 slices of bread, toasted

Mix mushrooms, onions, mustard, thyme and Parmesan cheese. Place on mixture on a slice of bread. Top with mustard and Monterey Jack cheese. Place under a broiler until cheese melts. Top with second slice of bread.

PORK OVERLOAD SANDWICHES

8 pork patties, tenderloin or ground pork
16 strips of bacon
8 onion ring slices
8 tomato slices
1 tablespoon of butter
Garlic powder to taste
Salt and pepper to taste
8 crusty rolls

Cross 2 strips of bacon and place the meat patty on top. Season the meat with salt, pepper and garlic powder. Cover with onion and tomato. Bring the bacon strips together and overlap the patty. Place on a broiling pan or a wire rack inside a roasting pan. Bake uncovered at 350 degrees for 50 to 60 minutes. Serve on crusty rolls.

REUBEN SLIDERS

1½ cups of corned beef, chopped
1 cup of sauerkraut
½ cup of shredded Swiss cheese
½ cup of Thousand Island dressing
1 loaf of thin-sliced cocktail rye

In a bowl combine corned beef, drained sauerkraut, shredded Swiss cheese and Thousand Island dressing. Mix well. Place mini-sandwiches on a baking sheet and bake at 375 degrees for 10 to 12 minutes or until cheese is melted.

SALAMI WRAPS

    1 package of dry salami slices
    1 can of chopped olives
    1 carton of whipped cream cheese
    Toothpicks

Mix cream cheese and chopped olives to your taste. Spread the mixture lightly in a salami piece. Roll up the salami and secure with a toothpick.

SLOPPY BUCK BBQ SANDWICH

1 pound of ground venison
1 cup of water
½ cup of celery
1 tablespoon of mustard
1 tablespoon of ketchup
Celery seed or celery salt
4 ounces of chili sauce

Cook venison in a pan with water and celery until the celery is tender. Add in chili sauce, mustard, ketchup and celery seed/salt to taste. Simmer uncovered for 30 minutes. Serve on toasted hamburger buns.

SPICY BBQ PORK SANDWICHES

1½ cups of spicy ketchup
    (or blend ketchup and hot sauce)
½ cup of onion, finely diced
¼ cup of green onion, finely diced
1 tablespoon of brown sugar
1 teaspoon of salt
1½ teaspoons of dry mustard
3½ cups of pork, cooked and shredded
Tabasco sauce to taste
Hamburger buns

Combine ketchup, onion, pepper, brown sugar, salt, mustard and Tabasco sauce in a pan. Cover and simmer for 15 minutes. Now add pork to sauce, cover and simmer for 10 minutes. Serve the mixture on toasted buns.

SPRITELY GOBBLE SANDWICH

4 turkey breast fillets
4 hoagie buns
1 cup of soy sauce
1 cup of Sprite
1 cup of cooking oil

Combine soy sauce, Sprite and oil. Marinate fillets overnight. Grill the meat 6 to 8 minutes per side until browned. Baste with the marinade while cooking.

TIKI BAR SANDWICH

2 slices of pumpernickel bread
5 slices of ham, sliced thin
1 slice of pineapple
3 ounces of mozzarella, sliced
¼ cup of basil leaves
2 teaspoons of olive oil

On the first slice of bread layer the ham, pineapple, mozzarella and basil. Drizzle oil over the basil leaves and top with second slice of bread.

TURKEY SOURDOUGH SANDWICH

Sourdough bread, thickly sliced
Turkey, thin-sliced white meat
Tomato, sliced thin
Guacamole
Mornay Sauce
Butter

Toast and butter the sourdough bread slices. Top with turkey, guacamole and sliced tomato. Top lightly with Mornay sauce.

TWO RIVERS MEATLOAF SANDWICH

2 pounds of ground elk
1 pound of ground beef
1 cup of water
1 package of dry onion soup mix
Hamburger buns

Combine all ingredients until well blended. Form into 2 loaves and bake uncovered in a loaf pan or baking dish at 350 degrees for 90 minutes. Let cool before slicing. Serve on hamburger buns with ketchup or hot sauce.

WALKING TACO

1 small bag of corn chips (Fritos work best)
½ pound of ground beef, cooked
1 onion chopped
2 tomatoes, chopped
1 cup of salsa
1½ cups of shredded cheese, taco blend

Open bag of chips slightly and crush chips in bag. Now open bag completely and mix in the ingredients, as you like. Sprinkle in hot sauce for the extra kick.

Cooking with Fire

Grill, Campfire and Foil Packets

APPLE DUMPLINGS

4 apples, peeled and cored
½ stick of butter, softened
¼ cup of brown sugar
1 teaspoon of apple pie spice
2 refrigerated pie dough rounds, cut in half

Mix butter, sugar and spice thoroughly and stuff into the core of each apple. Wrap pie dough half around each apple. Seal each apple up in a packet of non-stick aluminum foil. Grill over medium heat for 30 minutes, turning a few times.

BABY CARROTS

1 pound of baby carrots
1 shallot, chopped
1 pat of butter
1 teaspoon of tarragon
Salt and pepper

Put all of the ingredients in the center of heavy-duty foil. Form it into a packet. Grill over medium-high heat for 15 minutes.

BARBECUE PORK BURGER

2 pounds of ground pork
¼ cup fresh breadcrumbs
1 cup of barbecue sauce
6 hamburger buns
Salt and pepper (optional)
6 hamburger buns

Mix ground pork with breadcrumbs and ½ cup of sauce to make six patties. Grill burgers on medium high heat, basting burgers often with remaining sauce. Cook 4 to 5 minutes per side.

BEEF BARBECUE SANDWICHES

4 pounds of lean beef, cut into chunks
14 ounces of tomatoes, canned
2 medium onions, diced
1 quart of water
1 cup of ketchup
1 tablespoon of chili powder
½ cup of vinegar
½ cup of Worcestershire sauce
Salt and pepper to taste
Garlic powder to taste
Liquid smoke (optional)
Hamburger buns

Combine all ingredients in a Dutch oven. Simmer uncovered on low heat for 5 to 6 hours or until beef falls to shreds. The mixture should be thick. Spoon the beef mixture onto hoagie or crusty rolls.

BEEF JERKY CHILI

½ cup of chopped bacon
1 onion, chopped
2 cloves of garlic, minced
2 cups beef broth
4 chili peppers, chopped
2 tablespoons chili powder
2 tablespoons light brown sugar
1½ tablespoons of cumin
5 cups fresh tomatoes, peeled & chopped
½ tablespoon pepper
2½ cups of beef jerky, chopped
2½ cups kidney or pinto beans, cooked

Cook bacon in deep cast iron pot or Dutch oven until fat is released, but not crisp. Add onion and garlic and cook until tender. Add in chili peppers, tomatoes and broth. Cook until tomatoes are soft, 15 to 20 minutes. Now combine chili powder, brown sugar, cumin and pepper and then add to pot. Stir in the beef jerky. Simmer on a low boil for 45 minutes. Add beans last and boil for 5 minutes.

BEER CAN CHICKEN

4-pound chicken
3 tablespoons of oil
1 half can of beer, room temperature
1 tablespoon of kosher salt or sea salt
1 tablespoon of dried thyme
1 tablespoon of black pepper

Rub the chicken with oil. Mix salt, pepper, thyme and sprinkle over chicken. Fire up the grill. When it reaches temperature, put the half empty can of beer on the grill, set up for indirect heat. Put chicken over the can so it is sitting upright, with the can in the cavity. Cover the grill. After one hour, check the chicken and refresh coals if needed. Using a meat thermometer, check every 15 minutes until the thickest part of the thigh reaches 160 to 165 degrees.

BLT BURGER

1 pound of ground steak
½ pound of bacon, diced
1 onion, grated
3 cloves of garlic, crushed
2 teaspoons of oil
Tomato, sliced
Lettuce
4 hamburger buns

Mix bacon, steak, garlic and onion thoroughly together. Form into 4 patties and place in a refrigerator or in a Ziploc bag on ice for 1 hour. Oil the heated grill. Cook each burger for 4 to 6 minutes per side or to desired doneness. Top with lettuce and tomato. You can also cook in a cast iron skillet with a few tablespoons of oil.

BRATS ON A STICK

6 brats, cut into quarters
¼ cup of light cream
2 tablespoons of mustard
1 teaspoon of minced onion
¼ teaspoon of pepper
16 ounces of sauerkraut, drained
Hot sauce to taste (optional)
Pinch of paprika
4 sticks or skewers

Put brat pieces on 4 skewers. Make a sauce of the cream, mustard, onion, pepper, paprika and hot sauce. Grill brats over medium heat for 8 to 10 minutes. Turn and baste with liquid often. After you've heated the sauerkraut, place meat skewers on a bed of the kraut and pour sauce over everything.

BREAKFAST HASH

2 cups of meat (beef, chicken or ham) cooked and diced
2 cups copped cooked potatoes
1½ onions, minced
2 tablespoons parsley
1 cup of milk
Salt and pepper
Vegetable oil or Crisco

Mix all ingredients together except the milk. Place oil or Crisco in a cast iron skillet over fire or grill at medium heat. When hot, spread has mix evenly in skillet. Brown the bottom of hash quickly, 10 to 15 minutes. Now add milk and mix. Cover and cook slowly for about 10 minutes or until crisp.

CABIN POTATOES

5 cups of potatoes, sliced thin
¼ cup of oil (or bacon drippings)
1 onion, sliced thin
1 teaspoon of salt
1 teaspoon of parsley, chopped
Pepper to taste

Over a fire or on a grill, heat oil in a cast iron skillet over low heat. Drop in potatoes, onions, parsley, salt and pepper. Cover the skillet and cook for 15 minutes. Stir occasionally and re-cover. Remove cover after 15 minutes and cook for another 5 minutes until potatoes are brown.

CAJUN SHRIMP

1½ pounds of shrimp,
    shelled and deveined with tails
3 green onions, diced
3 cloves of garlic, minced
2 tablespoons of lemon juice
1 tablespoon of olive oil
2 teaspoons of paprika
1 teaspoon of salt
¼ teaspoon of pepper
½ teaspoon of cayenne pepper

Mix onion, lemon juice, garlic, paprika, salt, pepper and cayenne together thoroughly in a Ziploc bag and stir in the olive oil. Drop in the shrimp and coat completely. Let the shrimp marinade for 30 to 60 minutes in the bag on ice. Thread the shrimp onto skewers. Soaking wooden skewers in hot water for 30 minutes prevents burning. Brush the grill with oil and grill shrimp skewers for 2 to 3 minutes per side or until they become opaque.

CAMPERS MIX

2 pounds of flour
2 pounds of whole-wheat flour
1 pound of yellow corn meal
¾ pound of soy flour
¾ pound of wheat germ

Combine all five ingredients thoroughly. Seal in a watertight container. This mix works great for baking, coating and frying.

CAMPFIRE BURGERS

1 pound of hamburger
1 onion
2 carrots
2 potatoes
Salt and pepper to taste
4 hamburger buns

Make burger patties and place on aluminum foil. Thinly slice onions, carrots and potatoes and place on top of meat. Salt and pepper to taste. Fold foil into a pocket and fold edges over. Cook over the campfire.

CAMPFIRE COFFEE

1 cup of hot chocolate mix
1 cup of non-dairy creamer
½ cup instant coffee
½ teaspoon cinnamon
¼ teaspoon nutmeg
½ to ¾ cup sugar

Mix hot chocolate, creamer, coffee, cinnamon and nutmeg thoroughly. Add in sugar and blend well. Drop 3 to 4 heaping teaspoons into a mug and pour in hot water.

CAMPFIRE POTATOES

5 potatoes, sliced for French fries
1 onion, sliced thin
1 clove of garlic, sliced fine
¼ cup of oil
2 tablespoons of milk
Salt
Pepper

On a piece of heavy-duty aluminum foil, pile sliced potatoes in the middle. Add onion and garlic. Turn up the edges to prevent liquid from escaping. Pour oil over everything and season with salt and pepper. Crimp edges of the foil packet and seal securely. Place the packet on a grill grate 4 to 6 inches above hot coals. Potatoes should be done in 45 to 60 minutes.

CAMPFIRE SPLIT

1 banana
Peanut Butter
Milk chocolate bar
Mini-marshmallows

Peel half of the banana completely leaving skin attached at the bottom. Paint with peanut butter. Smash chocolate bar into small pieces and sprinkle some on the peanut butter along with mini-marshmallows. Replace the skin and double wrap in tin foil. Place the package on glowing embers, a grill or in a hot skillet for 8 to 10 minutes. Turn often.

CARIBBEAN TURKEY BURGER

1 pound of ground turkey
1 teaspoon of salt
1 tablespoon of pepper
1 tablespoon of thyme
4 teaspoons of allspice
1 habanero pepper, minced
4 scallions, chopped
4 slices of Muenster cheese
1 onion, sliced
1 tomato, sliced
1 mango, peeled and sliced
4 hamburger buns

Mix spices, habanero and scallions together to make the jerk seasoning. Mix ¼ cup of the seasoning with the ground turkey. Save remainder for future use. Make 4 patties from the meat. Grill on an oiled barbecue or in a frying pan. Put burgers on buns and top with cheese, onion, tomato and mango.

CAST IRON COOKIES

1 stick of butter
¾ cup of sugar
1 cup of dates, chopped (or raisins)
1 cup of pecans, chopped
1 cup of Rice Krispies
2 eggs, beaten
1 teaspoon of vanilla
1 ½ cup of coconut, shredded

In a cast iron skillet, slowly melt the butter over a campfire or grill. Stir in sugar. Add dates or raisins, vanilla and beaten eggs. Stir until thick. Let mixture cool and stir in Rice Krispies and nuts. Form into balls and roll in coconut.

CATFISH STEW

2 pounds of catfish fillets
6 slices of bacon
3 cups of potatoes, diced
1½ cups of onion, diced
28 ounces of canned tomatoes
8 ounces of tomato sauce
2 tablespoons of Worcestershire sauce
2 tablespoons of salt
Hot pepper sauce to taste (optional)
¼ teaspoon of pepper

Cut catfish into 1 to 2 inch pieces. Fry bacon in the Dutch oven until crisp. Remove bacon and drain on paper towels, crumble and set aside. Add onion to the Dutch oven, cover and cook in bacon grease for 5 minutes or until tender. Add in all ingredients except catfish and crumbled bacon. Bring pot to a boil then simmer for 30 minutes. Add bacon and catfish, cover, and simmer for 8 to 10 minutes.

CATFISH CAKES

1 pound of catfish fillets, cleaned
2½ cups of coarsely crushed crackers
1 cup of vegetable oil
1 onion, diced
1 egg
1 tablespoon of mayonnaise
1 teaspoon of yellow mustard
½ teaspoon of Old Bay seasoning

Boil catfish fillets in a pan until fish flakes easily. Drain the water and put fish in a bowl. Break into small pieces. Mix all the ingredients together except the oil. Form into 6 patties. Pour oil into a hot cast iron skillet and fry for 2 to 4 minutes per side or until lightly browned. Serve with a sauce of your choice on the side or on hamburger buns.

CHERRY ALMOND PORK CHOPS

4 pork chops, ½-inch thick
1 tablespoon of shortening
1 tablespoon of cider vinegar
16 ounces of pitted light cherries w/syrup
¼ cup of slivered almonds
6 whole cloves
Salt and pepper to taste

Brown pork chops in a cast iron skillet with shortening, season with salt and pepper. Mix cherries and syrup with almonds, cloves and vinegar. Drain shortening and pour cherry mixture over the chops. Simmer for 30 minutes.

CHICAGO-STYLE HOT DOGS

Hot Dogs
Poppy Seed buns
Dill pickle spears
Cucumber spears
Tomato slices
Pickled peppers
Diced onion
Mustard (yellow)
Sweet relish (electric green if available)
Celery salt

Grill or boil the hot dogs. Use soft, fresh poppy seed buns. Load up your dogs with all the ingredients starting with the celery salt.

CLAM FRITTERS

2 cups of clams, minced
2 cups of biscuit mix
2/3 cup of milk
1 egg
Oil

Combine biscuit mix, milk and egg and stir. The batter may turn out a little chunky. Over fire or on a grill, heat oil in a cast iron skillet or Dutch oven. Oil should get to 350 to 375 degrees. Stir clams into batter and carefully drop spoonfuls into the hot oil. Brown the fritters on both sides. Remove the oil and drain on paper towels.

CLASSIC BURGER

1 pound of ground beef
1 onion, finely diced
2 garlic cloves, crushed
2 tablespoons of brown mustard
2 tablespoons of oil
Pepper to taste
4 hamburger buns

Combine meat, onion, garlic, mustard and pepper and thoroughly mix. Form into 4 patties. Heat oil in a skillet and cook 3 to 6 minutes per side until burger reaches desired doneness. This also makes the perfect cheeseburger.

COLLARD GREENS

1 large bunch of collard greens
   (kale or chard can be used)
1 tablespoon of olive oil
3 cloves or garlic, minced
Juice from ½ a lemon
Salt and pepper to taste

Use the top portion of the greens and wash thoroughly. Cut leaves into strips and stack leaves on top of each other in a bowl. Heat oil in a cast iron skillet and sauté garlic for a few minutes until golden brown. Add greens to the pan and stir to coat. Stir frequently until the greens are tender. Depending on the greens it could take 3 to 8 minutes. Remove from heat and add lemon juice and vinegar. Salt and pepper to taste.

CRAWFISH STEW

3 cups of crawfish meat, cooked and cleaned
½ cup of shortening
¾ cup of flour
1 onion, diced
2 cloves of garlic, minced
1 stalk of celery, diced
1 pint of water
Salt and pepper to taste

In a cast iron pot or Dutch oven heat the shortening. Add flour and stir until browned. Add onion, garlic and celery and stir. Now drop in the crawfish meat and stir again. Add water, cover and simmer for 20 minutes.

CURSES, FOILED AGAIN FISH

4 fish fillets, ¼ pound to ½ pound each, cleaned and de-boned
1 onion, diced
1 stalk of celery (celery salt can be used)
1 green pepper, diced
4 pats of butter
Salt and pepper

Place each fillet on a piece of aluminum foil big enough to fully wrap each fish. Add in onion, green pepper and celery (or celery salt). Salt and pepper to taste. Top with a pat of butter. Wrap tightly and bake directly on hot coals or grill for 15 to 20 minutes. This makes for a great campfire dinner.

DEER CAMP CHILI

2 pounds of venison, ground
40 ounces of canned hot chili beans, drained
56 ounces of canned stewed tomatoes
6 ounces of tomato paste
1 onion, diced
4 jalapenos, sliced with seeds removed
6 stalks of celery, diced
1 tablespoon of red pepper flakes, crushed
1 teaspoon of salt
2 tablespoons of oil
White pepper

In a big pot, brown venison in oil over medium high heat. Add in onion, celery, jalapenos and red pepper flakes. Continue to sauté for 2 to 3 more minutes until onions are transparent. Now add beans, tomatoes with juice and tomato paste to the pot. Add salt and white pepper to taste. Reduce heat and simmer for 30 to 60 minutes.

DUTCH OVEN CAMP BREAKFAST

1 pound of venison, beef or sausage, ground
2 tablespoons of oil
1 small onion, diced
12 eggs
1 can of diced chilies (choose your heat)
1 pound of cheddar cheese, shredded

Pour oil in a Dutch oven then brown meat and onion. Pour off excess grease and season to taste. Break eggs into oven and add chilies. Stir over medium heat until eggs are nearly cooked. Sprinkle cheese over the top. Remove from heat put on lid to let cheese melt for a few minutes.

DUTCH OVEN CORN BREAD

2 eggs
1 cup of buttermilk
½ cup of flour
1½ cups of cornmeal
¼ cup of shortening
1 tablespoon of sugar
3 teaspoons of baking powder
1 teaspoon of salt
½ teaspoon of baking soda

Mix all ingredients thoroughly. Pour batter in a hot, greased Dutch oven. Cover with the lid and place hot coals on the lid. Check every 10 minutes to see when it's done.

FLOUNDER DINNER

2 pounds of flounder fillets, cut into chunks
1 pound of tomatoes, peeled & sliced
1½ cups of potatoes, diced
1 ½ cups of green beans, sliced
6 slices of bacon, diced
2 tablespoons of onion, diced fine
3 teaspoons of salt
Pepper to taste

Cut aluminum foil into 6 pieces, 18-inches long. Evenly distribute fish in the center of the foil pieces. Evenly distribute bacon, tomato, potato, onion and green beans. Season with salt and pepper. Wrap and seal securely. Place on hot coals for 20 minutes. Turn frequently for even cooking. This recipe works with a variety of fish.

FRUIT SOUP

¼ cup of raisins
½ cup of dried prunes
½ cup of dried apples
½ cup of mixed, dried fruit
½ cup of Orange Tang
3 ounces or raspberry gelatin
1 cinnamon stick
½ cup of powdered whole milk
1 cup of hot water
Pinch of salt

Put dried fruits in a Dutch oven. Fill with dried fruits and cover with water. Stir in salt, Tang, gelatin and the cinnamon stick. Bring to a boil, cover and reduce to a simmer for 20 minutes or until fruit is tender. Stir dry milk into a cup of hot water until dissolved then add to fruit and thoroughly mix.

GARLIC SHRIMP

1 pound of large shrimp, unpeeled
½ stock of butter, softened
1 cup of chopped parsley
2 cloves of garlic, minced
Juice from 1 lemon
¼ teaspoon of red pepper flakes
Salt and pepper to taste

Thoroughly mix butter, parsley, garlic salt and pepper. Divide mixture between 2 foil packets adding ½ pound to each. Firmly seal the packets and grill on high heat for 8 minutes.

GATOR STEW

3 pounds of alligator meat, diced
½ cup of oil
2 cups of diced onions
1 cup of diced celery
1 cup of diced bell pepper
2 tablespoons of chopped garlic
2 tablespoons of diced jalapenos
16 ounces of pinto beans (canned)
24 ounces of tomato sauce
1 cup of chicken stock
1 tablespoon of chili powder
1 tablespoon of cumin
Salt and pepper

In a large pot or Dutch oven, heat oil over medium to high heat. Add gator meat and cook for 20 minutes. Add in onions, celery, bell pepper, garlic and jalapenos and sauté until vegetables are wilted, about 3 to 5 minutes. Add in pinto beans, tomato sauce and chicken stock. Bring to a boil and reduce to a simmer. Add chili powder and cumin and stir well. Cook for one hour. Stir occasionally. Once the meat is tender season to taste with salt and pepper.

GRILLED DUCK

3 duck breasts, de-boned and cut into slices
   ¾-inch thick
½ cup of onion, diced
1 stick of butter
Aluminum foil

Lay out two, 2-foot lengths of aluminum foil on top of each other. Sprinkle onion on top of the foil. Put breast meat on the onions and pour melted butter over the duck. Gather the four corners of the foil together, leaving an opening at the top. Cook on a grill on high heat for 50 to 70 minutes.

GRILLED KING SALMON

1 king salmon, 12 to 14 pounds
Garlic salt
Salt
Pepper

Split the salmon and remove the backbone. Season the fish with salt, pepper and garlic salt. Place the cut side down on the grill. Place your grill grate 10 to 12 inches above hot coals. After 20 minutes the cut side should be nicely browned. Turn carefully and let roast for 3 to 4 hours. You might want to put some smoking chips on the coals during the cooking.

GRILLED SIRLOIN

4 sirloin steaks, 6 ounces each
2 teaspoons of peanut oil

Herb butter:
1 sticks of unsalted butter
1 tablespoons of dill weed
½ tablespoon of fresh parsley, chopped
1 clove of garlic, minced
1 drop of lemon oil
Salt
Dry mustard

Combine all of the herb butter ingredients thoroughly and chill. Lightly coat steaks with peanut oil. Put meat on a hot grill for 8 to 10 minutes. Turn steaks and grill for 6 to 8 minutes more. Cut into center to test for doneness. Serve with herb butter.

HUEVOS RANCHEROS

2 tablespoons cooking oil
1 green or red pepper, finely chopped
1 small onion chopped
1 clove garlic, minced (optional)
1 teaspoon of chili powder
8 ounces tomato sauce
1 pound tomatoes, chopped
6 eggs
Salt and pepper

Over a campfire grate or on a grill, heat cooking oil in a large cast iron skillet and sauté pepper, onion and garlic until mushy. Stir in chili powder, tomato sauce and tomatoes. Cook until bubbly. Lower heat and season with salt and pepper to taste. Drops eggs into hot sauce and simmer over low heat, covered, until eggs are firm.

JALAPENO POPPERS

8 jalapeno chilies
Muenster cheese
¼ teaspoon of ground cumin
¼ teaspoon of ground coriander
Olive Oil
Salt

Remove the stems from the peppers and hollow them out, removing seeds and pulp. Stuff with Muenster cheese. Toss peppers with olive oil, salt to taste, cumin and coriander. Put everything in the middle of a piece of heavy-duty foil or double-upped foil. Fold edges and form a packet. Grill over medium-high heat for 10 minutes.

HONEY-LIME CHICKEN

4 chicken breasts, boneless and skinless
½ cup of honey
½ cup of soy sauce
¼ cup of lime juice, fresh squeezed

Put honey, soy sauce and lime juice in a Ziploc bag and mix thoroughly. Add chicken to the bag and mix to coat each breast. Seal the bag and refrigerate for 1 hour or stuff in an ice chest and surround bag with cubes. Remove chicken from the marinade. Grill the chicken over medium heat for 6 to 7 minutes per side.

ISLAND STEAK

1½ pounds of top sirloin steak
½ cup of soy sauce
¼ cup of brown sugar
2 tablespoons of olive oil
1 teaspoon of dry ginger
½ teaspoon of MSG
¼ teaspoon of pepper
2 cloves of minced garlic

Combine all ingredients, except the meat, and mix well. Cut the steak into 1-inch strips about ¼-inch thick. Add sauce to the meat and stir well to thoroughly coat. Marinade for two hours on ice or in the refrigerator. Place meat on skewers then grill.

LAMB BURGER

2 pounds of ground lamb
1 cup of breadcrumbs
½ cup of tomato sauce
1 tablespoon of vinegar
1 tablespoon of sugar
1 tablespoon of garlic salt
1 teaspoon of dry mustard
1 teaspoon of lemon juice
6 to 8 hamburger buns

Massage seasonings into the ground lamb, except the red pepper, and shape burgers lightly. Handle the meat as little as possible. Shape into 6 to 8 patties. Grill on a lightly oiled grate or fry in a cast iron skillet. After cooking, sprinkle the meat with red pepper.

LEMON HERB CHICKEN

1 chicken breast, skinless and boneless
2 tablespoons of mixed herbs, chopped
1 tablespoon of olive oil
1 tablespoon of lemon juice

Mix herbs, oil and juice together thoroughly. Coat the chicken with the mixture and seal up in an aluminum foil packet. Grill over medium-high heat for 12 minutes.

MEAT KABOBS

2 pounds of lamb or beef, cubed
5 cloves of garlic, minced
2 tablespoons of olive oil
2 tablespoons of ketchup
Salt and pepper to taste

Mix together ketchup garlic, ketchup, olive oil, salt and pepper to taste. Marinate the bite-sized meat cubes in sauce in a Ziploc bag on ice or in the refrigerator for 2 hours. Place meat on skewers over campfire coals or on a grill until done to taste. For different flavors, you can substitute yogurt for ketchup.

MUSHROOMS & SCALLOPS

¼ pound of fresh scallops
¼ pound of fresh mushrooms, sliced
2 tablespoons of butter
1 tablespoon of parsley, minced

Place ingredients in a piece of heavy-duty foil and double seal the ends. Place on hot coals for 10 to 12 minutes.

MUSTARD DILL SALMON

1 salmon fillet
4 lemon slices
Whole grain mustard
Brown sugar
Coriander, ground
Dill
Salt

On a piece of heavy-duty foil, layer lemon slices and fish then sprinkle with dill. Next, sprinkle brown sugar, salt followed by ground coriander. Spread mustard on last. Fold foil into a packet and grill over medium heat for 12 minutes.

NEW MEXICO CHICKEN

1 pound chicken breast, skinless & boneless
1 clove of garlic, pressed
2 tablespoons of olive oil
1 teaspoon of cumin, ground
1 teaspoon of chili powder
1 teaspoon of oregano
½ teaspoon of salt

Mix oil, garlic, cumin, chili powder, oregano and salt thoroughly. Coat both sides of the chicken with the mixture. Grill over medium heat for 8 to 10 minutes or until chicken is no longer pink in the center.

OATMEAL WITH APPLES

2 cups of water
2 apples, cored, peeled and grated
1 cup of rolled oats
½ teaspoon of salt
½ teaspoon of cinnamon

Put your pot over the fire or n the grate. Mix water, oats and salt and bring to a boil. Cover the pot (or Dutch oven) and let simmer for 10 minutes. Stir in apples and cinnamon, cover and cook for 10 more minutes.

POLISH SAUSAGE IN BEER

12 ounces of beer (1 can)
1 pound of Polish sausage a.k.a. Kielbasa
Juice from 1 lemon
Oil

Pour beer in a cast iron skillet. Heat to boiling over fire or grill then reduce heat. Pierce the sausage with a fork and poach the sausage for 4 minutes per side in the beer and drain. Brush the grate lightly with oil. Grill over medium heat 5 minutes per side. Just before serving, split sausage down the center and sprinkle with lemon juice.

PORTOBELLO MUSHROOMS

4 Portobello mushroom caps
4 garlic cloves, crushed
¼ cup of olive oil
1 teaspoon of red pepper flakes
Salt to taste
Parsley to taste, chopped

Toss all ingredients together and divide equally between 4 foil packets. Grill over medium heat for 10 minutes, turning after 5 minutes.

QUESADILLA

Flour tortillas, 8 or 10-inch
Chicken or pork, cooked and shredded
Pepper Jack cheese
Cilantro

On a piece of aluminum foil, place a tortilla. Sprinkle cheese on half of the tortilla, top with meat and sprinkle with cilantro. Fold tortilla in half and seal up in foil, keeping everything flat. Grill over medium heat for five minutes, flipping half through cooking.

ROOT BEER CHICKEN

4 6-ounce boneless chicken breast halves
2 tablespoons of oil
1 cup of root beer
½ cup of packed brown sugar
¼ cup of ketchup
4 teaspoons of Dijon mustard
2 teaspoons of lemon peel, grated

Flatten chicken breasts slightly. Pour oil into a cast iron skillet and cook 4 to 6 minutes each side or until meat thermometer reaches 170 degrees. Remove from skillet and keep warm. Into the skillet add root beer, brown sugar, ketchup, mustard and lemon peel. Bring to a boil for 6 to m8 minutes and stir until the sauce thickens. Return chicken to the skillet and heat thoroughly.

SALMON STEAKS

4 salmon steaks, 1-inch thick
½ cup of barbecue sauce
3 tablespoons of lemon juice
2 tablespoons of soy sauce
Salt and pepper to taste

Rinse the fish and pat dry. Combine soy sauce and lemon juice. Soak the salon in the liquid for 20 minutes while turning frequently. Remove the salmon and salt and pepper to taste. Oil the grill and cook fish over medium heat for 10 to 15 minutes. Halfway through cooking, turn the steaks and brush with barbecue sauce. When fish flakes it is done.

SEAFOOD POT

1 quart of water
7 cups of tomatoes, diced large
1 pound of scallops
1 pound of rockfish, cut into chunks
1 pound of shrimp, cleaned
12 slices of bacon, diced
1 cup of onion, diced
1 cup of celery, diced
½ onion, sliced
1 clove of garlic, diced
½ cup of sherry
¼ cup of ketchup
4 tablespoons of butter
1 tablespoon of Worcestershire sauce
2 teaspoons of salt
¼ teaspoon of curry powder
Tabasco sauce to taste

In a Dutch oven or large kettle, sauté bacon. Add onion and celery and cook for 5 minutes. Stir in water, lemon slices, garlic tomato, ketchup, curry powder, salt, Worcestershire and Tabasco and mix thoroughly. Cook for 30 minutes. Add scallops, fish, shrimp, wine and butter and cook for 10 minutes. When fish flakes it's ready to serve.

SHORE LUNCH TROUT

4 trout, cleaned
Salt & pepper
Dill (optional)
Garlic salt (optional)

Place cleaned fish on aluminum foil. Season to taste. Wrap fish in aluminum foil. If using lightweight foil, you may have to double or triple wrap. Place the foil packets on hot coals for 15 to 20 minutes, depending the size of the fish.

SKILLET BEANS

1 pound of fresh mushrooms, sliced thin
2 cans of red kidney beans
½ green pepper, sliced thin
1 onion, sliced thin
3 tablespoons of butter
1 tablespoon of salt
1 teaspoon of chili powder
1 clove of garlic, minced
¼ teaspoon of pepper

On a grill or over a fire, sauté mushrooms, green peppers and onion in butter in a cast iron skillet. Season with garlic and chili pepper to taste then salt and pepper. Add kidney beans and heat and stir until cooked.

SMELT ON THE COALS

6 whole smelt, gutted
6 strips of bacon, diced
1 tablespoon of lemon juice
1 tablespoon of parsley, chopped
Pinch of garlic powder
Salt and pepper to taste

Dip smelt in cold, salted water and pat dry. Over the campfire, fry bacon, parsley and onion in a cast iron skillet. Stir in lemon juice, garlic powder, salt and pepper to taste. Place smelt in the center of a large piece of aluminum foil. Rub each smelt with the bacon mixture and stuff remaining seasoning inside the fish cavities. Wrap each fish in foil, sealing the edges completely. Set foil packets in medium coals. Cook for 15 minutes, turning a few times.

S'MORES POPCORN

¼ cup of popcorn kernels
1 tablespoon of oil
Salt (optional)
2 tablespoons of cocoa powder
¼ cup of powdered sugar
¼ cup of graham crack crumbs
¼ cup of mini-marshmallows

Put oil and popcorn in the bottom of a disposable pie tin. Seal the tin with foil in the shape of a large dome. Think of it as a rustic Jiffy Pop. Grill over high heat until popping stops, about 8 minutes. You can salt here and eat basic popcorn. To turn it into S'mores, toss the warm popcorn in a bowl with remaining ingredients.

SNOW PEAS

½ pound of snow peas, trimmed
1 clove of garlic
2 tablespoons of oil
2 tablespoons of tomato juice
2 tablespoons of soy sauce
2 tablespoons of brown sugar
Pepper to taste

Combine garlic, oil, tomato juice, soy sauce, brown sugar and pepper in a bowl and mix thoroughly. Add in the snow peas and toss to coat. Let rest for 30 minutes. Place everything in a piece of heavy-duty aluminum shaped into a bowl or a foil pan. Place the foil/pan on the grid over high direct heat and cook for 10 to 15 minutes. Toss occasionally until crisp yet tender.

SQUIRREL STEW

2 squirrels, cleaned and cut into pieces
4 potatoes, cut into quarters
4 onions, sliced
1 pound of chopped carrots
1 green pepper, chopped
¼ head of cabbage
1 teaspoon of salt
1 teaspoon of ground black pepper
2 cups of water

Place all ingredients in a Dutch oven over the campfire and salt and pepper to taste. Cover and cook on low for eight hours.

SUMMER BURGER

1 pound of ground beef
1 teaspoon of salt
3 tablespoons of ketchup
1 teaspoon of mustard
1 teaspoon of horseradish
1 teaspoon of Worcestershire sauce
2 tablespoons of onion, diced
½ cup of breadcrumbs
¼ cup of milk
2 tablespoons of oil
Hamburger buns

Combine all ingredients except the oil. Shape into 4 to 8 patties. Oil the grill grate or pour oil into skillet and fry patties 4 to 6 minutes per side, depending on desired doneness.

TURKEY CHILI BURGER

1 pound of fresh ground turkey
¼ cup of chili sauce
1 teaspoon of chicken flavor bouillon powder
2 tablespoons of oil
4 hamburger buns

Combine all ingredients thoroughly except oil. Form into 4 patties and grill 4 to 6 minutes per side until desired doneness. If cooking on a barbecue, brush oil on the grate. If using a skillet, heat oil in it before cooking patties.

VEGETABLE SOUP

3 potatoes, cubed
2 carrots, sliced
1 large can of mixed vegetables, drained
1 small can of green peas, drained
15 ounces of tomato sauce
12 ounces of tomato juice
2 cloves of garlic, crushed
1 onion, finely chopped
2 cups of water
1 tablespoon of salt

Combine all ingredients in a cast iron pot or Dutch oven. Bring to a boil and reduce heat. Simmer over medium low heat for 45 minutes.

VENISON & MUSHROOMS

2 pounds of venison
1 can of mushroom soup
1 can of water
1 can of mushrooms, sliced
Flour
Oil
Salt and pepper to taste

Slice the meat into thin strips, dredge in flour and brown with a little oil in a Dutch oven. Once the venison is browned, add 1 can of mushroom soup, 1 can of water and 1 can of mushrooms. Cover the oven and simmer for 1 ½ to 2 hours. Stir frequently to avoid scorching.

VENISON IN THE POT

2 pounds of venison (elk steak works too)
1 cup of water
3 tablespoons of oil
1 cup of onion, diced
¾ cup of ketchup
½ cup of vinegar
½ cup of brown sugar
1 tablespoon of mustard
1 tablespoon of Worcestershire sauce
½ teaspoon of salt
¼ teaspoon of pepper

Cut steak into pieces and place into the Dutch oven with oil. Over the campfire, heat and brown meat on both sides. Remove the from the oven meat, add onion and brown. Add remaining ingredients to make the sauce and simmer for 5 minutes. Return meat to the pot, cover and cook over fire for 2 hours or until steak is tender.

Slow Cooker Recipes

ALL-DAY STEW

1½ pounds of beef, venison or elk, cubed
1 can of cream of mushroom soup
2 cans of golden mushroom soup
6 carrots, chopped
1 cup of celery, chopped
4 potatoes, chopped
1 package of Lipton's Onion Soup mix

Put ingredients in a cooker, cover and cook on low for 8 to 10 hours.

APPLESAUCE

10 apples, peeled, cored and sliced
½ cup of water
½ cup of sugar
½ cup of brown sugar
2 tablespoons of cinnamon
1 teaspoon of nutmeg
½ teaspoon of ground cloves
1 tablespoon of butter
2 tablespoons of lemon juice

Place ingredients in the cooker and stir thoroughly. Cover and cook on low for 8 to 10 hours. Chill the sauce upon completion or spoon the warm mixture on vanilla ice cream.

BACON CHEESE DIP

1 pound of bacon, diced
1 pound of cream cheese, softened and cubed
4 cups of Cheddar cheese, shredded
1 cup of half & half
2 teaspoons of Worcestershire sauce
1 teaspoon of dried onion, minced
½ teaspoon of dry mustard
½ teaspoon of salt
Tabasco sauce to taste (optional)

Brown bacon in a pan, drain and set aside. Put remaining ingredients in the cooker, cover and cook on low for 1 hour stirring occasionally until cheese is completely melted. Stir in bacon and cook for a few more minutes.

BAKED CHICKEN

3 pounds of chicken pieces
1 teaspoon of paprika
Salt and pepper

Make three 3-inch balls of aluminum foil and place them at the bottom of the crock-pot. Place chicken on top of the foil. Sprinkle with salt, pepper and paprika. Cover and cook on high for 1 hour, then switch to low for 8 to 10 hours.

BAKED OATMEAL

2 cups of dry quick oats
½ cup of sugar
1 egg, beaten
1½ teaspoons of baking powder
½ teaspoon of salt
¾ cup of milk
¼ cup of oil

Pour oil into the cooker to coat the bottom and sides. Add ingredients into the cooker and mix thoroughly. Cover and bake on low for 2½ to 3 hours.

BANANA BREAD

¾ cup of butter or margarine
1½ cups of sugar
1½ cups of mashed banana
½ cup of milk
2 eggs beaten
2 cups of flour
1 teaspoon of baking soda
¾ teaspoon of salt
½ cup walnuts, chopped (optional)

Combine ingredients and mix well to make a batter. Pour the batter into a greased and floured clean coffee can or similar metal container. Fill the container 2/3 full with batter. Make sure it fits loosely in the cooker. Cover the top of the can with 4 paper towels. Do not put water in the cooker. Put can in the cooker and put the lid on the cooker. Make sure the lid is slightly askew so excess moisture can escape. Cook on high for 4 hours.

BARBECUED CHICKEN

2 pounds of chicken pieces
2 cups of water
1 cup of ketchup
¼ cup of flour
¼ cup of Worcestershire sauce
1 teaspoon of chili powder
½ teaspoon of salt
½ teaspoon of pepper
¼ teaspoon of garlic salt
¼ teaspoon of onion salt
Tabasco sauce to taste

Dust the chicken pieces with flour and place in the cooker. Combine the rest of the ingredients in a bowl, mix thoroughly and pour over chicken. Pout the cover on and cook on low for 5 hours.

BARBECUED GAME STEAK

2 pounds of venison or elk steak
1 cup of water
3 tablespoons of oil
1 cup of onion, diced
¾ cup of ketchup
½ cup of vinegar
½ cup of brown sugar
1 tablespoon of mustard
1 tablespoon of Worcestershire sauce
½ teaspoon of salt
¼ teaspoon of pepper

Cut steak into pieces and place into Dutch oven with oil. Heat and brown meat on both sides. Remove the meat, add onion and brown. Add remaining ingredients to make the sauce cover and simmer for 5 minutes. Return meat to the pot and bake for 2 hours or until steak is tender.

BARBECUED HAM

2 pounds of ham, cubed
2 cups of cola
2 cups of ketchup

Place ham in the cooker and pour cola and ketchup over the meat. Cover and cook on low for 8 hours. Serve on hamburger or hot dog buns.

BARBECUED HOT DOGS

2 pounds of hot dogs, cut into 1-inch pieces
1 cup of apricot preserves
4 ounces of tomato sauce
¼ cup of vinegar
2 tablespoons of soy sauce
2 tablespoons of honey
1 tablespoon of oil
1 teaspoon of salt
¼ teaspoon of fresh ground ginger

Combine all of the ingredients in the cooker except the hot dogs. Stir, cover and cook on high for 30 minutes. Add hot dogs and reduce heat to low. Cover and cook for 4 hours.

BARBECUED RIBLETS

4 pounds of country-style ribs,
 cut into bite-sized pieces
1 can of tomato soup
½ cup of apple cider vinegar
½ cup of brown sugar
1 tablespoon of soy sauce
1 teaspoon of celery seed
1 teaspoon of salt
1 teaspoon of chili powder
Cayenne pepper to taste

Place ribs in the cooker. Mix remaining ingredients together thoroughly and pour over the meat. Cover and cook on low for 6 to 8 hours.

BEEF & GREEN BEANS

3 pounds of beef, cut into chunks
1 pound of frozen green beans
1 can of stewed tomatoes
1 onion, sliced into rings
1 tablespoon of paprika
1 tablespoon of Worcestershire sauce
1 teaspoon of garlic salt
1 teaspoon of garlic juice
Pepper to taste

Place ingredients in the cooker, cover and cook on low for 8 to 10 hours.

BEEF BARBECUE

4 pounds of lean beef, cut into chunks
14 ounces of tomatoes, canned
2 medium onions, diced
1 quart of water
1 cup of ketchup
1 tablespoon of chili powder
½ cup of vinegar
½ cup of Worcestershire sauce
Salt and pepper to taste
Garlic powder to taste
Liquid smoke (optional)
Hamburger buns

Combine all ingredients in a Dutch oven. Simmer uncovered on low heat for 5 to 6 hours or until beef falls to shreds. The mixture should be thick. Spoon onto hamburger buns.

BEEF ROAST

3 pound beef roast
1 envelope of dry onion soup mix
14 ounces of stewed tomatoes, canned

Put roast in the cooker and cover with onion soup and tomatoes. Cover and cook on low for 8 hours.

BEEF STEW

2 pounds of beef, cubed
3 potatoes, diced
1½ cups of beef broth
4 carrots, sliced
2 onions, diced
1 stalk of celery, diced
1 teaspoon of Worcestershire sauce
½ cup of flour
½ clove of garlic, minced
1½ teaspoons of salt
1 teaspoon of paprika
½ teaspoon of pepper
1 bay leaf

Place meat in the bottom of the cooker. Combine flour, salt, pepper and paprika and stir into the meat until all the cubes are coated. Add remaining ingredients and mix thoroughly. Cover and cook on low for 10 to 12 hours. Remove bay leaf before serving.

BEEF STROGANOFF

1 pound of round steak
1 cup of onions, diced
1 cup of beef broth
¼ cup of flour
8 ounces of mushrooms, canned or fresh
1 clove or garlic, minced
1 tablespoon of Dijon mustard
2 teaspoons of parsley
½ teaspoon of salt
¼ teaspoon of pepper
Egg noodles

Put steak, mushrooms, onion, mustard, dill, garlic, salt and pepper into the cooker. Mix beef broth and flour together. If mixture seems a little thin, add an additional teaspoon or two of flour. Pour the mixture into the cooker. Put on the cover and cook on low for 8 hours. Prepare noodles according to package directions and serve stroganoff over the noodles.

BEER BRATS

6 bratwurst, fresh not frozen
2 cloves or garlic, minced
2 tablespoons of olive oil
12 ounces of beer (1 can)

Brown meat in a pan with garlic and olive oil. Pierce casings of the sausages with a fork and cook for 5 more minutes. Put meat in the cooker and pour in the beer. Cover and cook on low for 6 to 7 hours.

BIG CHUNK O'BEEF

3 pounds of brisket or roast
4 potatoes, peeled and diced
4 carrots, cleaned and sliced
2 onions, diced
10 ounces of beef bouillon
1 cup of water
½ cup of red wine
2 tablespoons of parsley
1 tablespoon of Worcestershire sauce
2 teaspoons of salt
¼ teaspoon of pepper
1 bay leaf

Place vegetables in the cooker followed by meat, spices and liquid. Top with bay leaf so it's easy to remove after cooking. Cover and cook on low for 8 to 10 hours.

BIG GAME CHICKEN WINGS

5 pounds of chicken wings
28 ounces of tomato or spaghetti sauce
1 tablespoon of Worcestershire sauce
1 tablespoon of molasses
1 tablespoon of mustard
1 teaspoon of salt
½ teaspoon of pepper

Place wings in the cooker. Combine ingredients and pour over wings. Stir gently making sure each wing is coated. Cover and cook on high for 3 to 4 hours.

BOLOGNA & SAUERKRAUT

32-ounce bag of sauerkraut, rinsed
1 large ring bologna
1/3 cup of brown sugar

Combine sauerkraut and brown sugar in the cooker and stir. Remove casing from bologna and cut into ¼-inch slices. Add to the sauerkraut and stir. Cover and cook on low for 6 to 8 hours.

BRUNSWICK STEW

1 pound of skinless, boneless chicken, diced
2 potatoes, sliced thin
1 can of tomato soup
16 ounces of stewed tomatoes, canned
10 ounces of frozen corn
10 ounces of frozen lima beans
3 tablespoons of onion flakes
¼ teaspoon of salt
Pepper to taste

Combine all the ingredients in the cooker. Cover and cook on high for 2 hours then reduce to low for 2 more hours.

CATFISH STEW

2 pounds of catfish fillets
6 slices of bacon
3 cups of potatoes, diced
1½ cups of onion, diced
28 ounces of canned tomatoes
8 ounces of tomato sauce
2 tablespoons of Worcestershire sauce
2 tablespoons of salt
Hot pepper sauce to taste (optional)
¼ teaspoon of pepper

Cut fresh or thawed catfish into 1 to 2 inch pieces. Fry bacon in the Dutch oven until crisp. Remove bacon and drain on paper towels, crumble and set aside. Add onion to the Dutch oven, cover and cook in bacon grease for 5 minutes or until tender. Add in all ingredients except catfish and crumbled bacon. Bring pot to a boil then simmer for 30 minutes. Add bacon and catfish, cover, and simmer for 8 to 10 minutes.

CHICKEN & MUSHROOMS

6 boneless, skinless chicken breast halves
1 can of cream of mushroom soup
4 ounces of sliced mushrooms,
   (If using canned mushrooms, drain liquid)
¼ cup of chicken broth
Salt and pepper to taste

Place chicken in the cooker and season with salt and pepper. Combine chicken broth and soup and pour over chicken then top with mushrooms. Cover and cook on low for 7 to 9 hours.

CHICKEN GUMBO

2 pounds of boneless chicken breasts, cubed
2 pounds of okra, cut to ¼-inch slices
2 stalks of celery, diced
3 tomatoes, diced
2 onions, diced
2 bell peppers, diced
4 tablespoons of oil
3 tablespoons of flour
2 cloves of garlic, minced
1 quart of water
Salt and pepper to taste

Heat Dutch oven to 325 degrees and add oil and flour. Stir until flour browns. Add garlic, onion and bell peppers. Slowly stir in 1 quart of water. Add salt and pepper to taste followed by celery, okra and tomatoes. Heat to boiling then reduce to 225 degrees. Cover and simmer for 30 minutes and vegetables are cooked. Add chicken and simmer for another 20 minutes or until chicken is cooked.

CHICKEN POTATO CASSEROLE

1 chicken in parts
5 potatoes
1 can of cream of chicken soup
½ cup of green onions, chopped
½ can of water
Salt and pepper

Brown the chicken in a frying pan. In the Dutch oven, slice potatoes and salt and pepper to taste. Add green onions and place chicken on top. Mix soup with ½ can of water and pour over the top. Cover and bake for 60 to 90 minutes. Check during the last 30 minutes for doneness.

CHICKEN REUBEN POT

2 boneless, skinless chicken breasts cut in half
2 pounds of sauerkraut, rinsed and drained
4 slices of Swiss cheese
1¼ cups of Thousand Island salad dressing
2 tablespoons of fresh parsley, chopped

Put chicken in the cooker. Put sauerkraut over chicken and top with cheese. Pour salad dressing over the cheese and sprinkle with parsley. Cover and cook on low for 6 to 8 hours.

CHILI CHEESE DIP

1 pound of ground beef
½ cup of onion, diced
1 cup of Velveeta cheese, diced
5 ounces of tomatoes, diced
5 ounces of green chilies, diced
1 can of evaporated milk
Salt and pepper to taste

Brown ground beef in a pan with a little oil. Drain the grease and season with salt and pepper. Combine all the ingredients in the cooker, stir then cover. Set to low and cook for 4 hours. Stir every 45 minutes. This is the perfect dip for tailgating and football parties.

CHILI NUTS

24 ounces of canned cocktail peanuts
¼ cup of melted butter
Chili seasoning mix to taste

In the cooker, pour melted butter over the nuts. Sprinkle chili-seasoning mix over the nuts and toss. Cover and cook on low for 2 hours. Turn to high for 15 minutes. Remove lid and serve.

CHILI WITH BEANS

2 large cans of kidney beans, drained
2 pounds of ground beef
32 ounces of canned tomatoes
1 can of tomato paste
1 bell pepper, diced
1 onion, diced
3 tablespoons of chili powder
2 cloves of garlic, minced
Tabasco sauce to taste

Brown the meat in a skillet and drain. Add all ingredients to the slow cooker and stir. Cover and cook on low for 10 to 12 hours.

CLAM CHOWDER

30 ounces of cream of potato soup, canned
20 ounces of clam chowder, canned
12 ounces of canned clams, chopped
½ cup of butter
1 onion, diced
1 pint of half & half

Combine all the ingredients in the cooker. Cover and cook on low for 2 to 4 hours.

COLA BEEF

3 pounds of beef roast
24 ounces of cola (2 cans)
1 envelope of dry onion soup mix

Put roast in the cooker. Sprinkle with soup mix and pour cola all over the meat. Cover and cook on low for 7 to 8 hours.

COLA CHICKEN

4 boneless chicken breasts
1 can of cola
1 cup of ketchup
1 cup of barbecue sauce

Cut chicken breasts into strips. Mix cola, barbecue sauce and ketchup together in a Dutch oven. Heat to 350 degrees stirring continuously until it reaches that point. Drop in chicken strips and put on the lid. Cook for 45 minutes making sure to stir every 5 to 10 minutes. When chicken is done, serve on a bed of noodles or rice.

COLCANNON

6 potatoes, peeled and cubed
2 cups of cabbage, chopped
1 onion, diced
1 tablespoon of butter
½ teaspoon of salt
Pepper to taste
Water

Put potatoes in a Dutch oven and cover with water. Bring to a boil. Cover and cook over medium heat for 8 to 10 minutes, until potatoes are almost tender. Add cabbage and onion, cover and simmer for 5 minutes or until cabbage is tender. Drain well and mash with butter, salt and pepper.

CORNED BEEF

3 carrots, cleaned and chunked
3 pounds of corned beef brisket
2 onions, sliced into quarters
2 celery tops
1 turnip, sliced into chunks
3 potatoes, diced large

In the slow cooker, place layers of each ingredient in the order listed. Fill with water to about 1-inch from the top. Cover and cook on low for 8 to 10 hours.

CRAB SOUP

1 pound of crabmeat
1 pound of ham, diced
1 pound of beef, diced
6 slices of bacon, diced
1 pound of carrots, sliced
1 onion, diced
3 stalks of celery, diced
20 ounces of frozen mixed vegetables
12 ounces of tomato juice
1 tablespoon of Old Bay seasoning
1 teaspoon of salt
¼ teaspoon of pepper
Water

Put all ingredients in the cooker except crabmeat and seasonings. Pour in enough water so cooker is half-full. Add seasonings, stir thoroughly and put crab on top. Cover and cook on low for 8 to 10 hours. Stir well before serving.

CRANBERRY CHICKEN

3 pounds of chicken parts
16 ounces of cranberry sauce, berry not jelly
1 cup of barbecue sauce
½ cup of celery, diced
½ cup of onion, diced
½ teaspoon of salt
½ teaspoon of pepper

Put chicken in the cooker. Mix ingredients together thoroughly and pour over the parts. Cover and cook on low for 6 to 8 hours.

CREAMY RED POTATOES

2 pounds of small red potatoes, quartered
8 ounces of cream cheese, softened
1 10-ounce can of potato soup
1 package of dry Ranch salad dressing

Put potatoes in a slow cooker. Mix cream cheese, soup and Ranch dressing together and stir into potatoes. Cover and cook on low for 8 hour or until potatoes are tender.

CROCK-POT PIZZA

1 pound of Italian sausage, browned, sliced and drained
28 ounces of tomatoes, diced (canned or fresh)
16 ounces of chili beans, canned
2 ounces of canned black olives, chopped
1 medium onion, diced
1 green pepper, diced
2 cloves of garlic, minced
¼ cup of Parmesan cheese, grated
1 tablespoon of quick-cooking tapioca
1 tablespoon of basil
1 teaspoon of salt
Mozzarella cheese, shredded

Combine all ingredients in the cooker except mozzarella cheese. Stir thoroughly. Cover and cook on low for 8 to 9 hours. When serving, top with mozzarella cheese. Tastes great on pasta, rice or in a wrap.

DUTCH OVEN CAMP BREAKFAST

1 pound of venison, ground
2 tablespoons of oil
1 small onion, diced
12 eggs
1 can of diced chilies (choose your heat)
1 pound of cheddar cheese, shredded

Pour oil in a Dutch oven then brown venison and onion. Pour off excess grease and season to taste. Break eggs into oven and add chilies. Stir over medium heat until eggs are nearly cooked. Sprinkle cheese over the top. Remove from heat put on lid to let cheese melt for a few minutes.

ELK & KRAUT

3 potatoes, diced
1 ½ pounds of elk, ground
1 jar or can of sauerkraut, drained
 (12 to 16 ounces works)
1 cup of water
1 cup of croutons
1 onion, diced
1 egg, beaten
3 tablespoons of oil
2 tablespoons of brown sugar
2 tablespoons of salt
2 tablespoons of ketchup, barbecue sauce or chili sauce (choose to taste)
1 tablespoon of pepper

Heat oil in a Dutch oven. Add in all your ingredients and stir a few times. Put on the lid and leave it alone for 90 minutes to let the flavors blend. If cooking over a fire, too much heat will make the ingredients stick to the inside of the oven. Check for doneness after 90 minutes. If not cooked, check every 10 to 15 minutes.

GEORGIA RIBS

4 pounds of boneless pork ribs
15 ounces of canned spiced cling peaches, diced with juice
½ cup of brown sugar
¼ cup of ketchup
¼ cup of white vinegar
1 garlic clove, minced
2 tablespoons of soy sauce
1 teaspoon of salt
1 teaspoon of pepper

Cut ribs into bite-sized pieces. Brown in a pan with a little oil. Drain and put meat in the cooker. Combine remaining ingredients in a bowl and mix thoroughly. Pour over the ribs, cover and cook on low for 8 to 10 hours.

GLAZED CARROTS

2 pounds of baby carrots
½ cup of brown sugar
½ cup of fresh squeezed orange juice
3 tablespoons of butter
¾ teaspoon of cinnamon
¼ teaspoon of nutmeg
2 tablespoons of cornstarch
¼ cup of water

Combine all but the final 2 ingredients and place in a slow cooker. Cover and cook on low for 3 to 4 hours. Carrots should be tender but crisp, not mushy. Pour of the juice into a small pan. Put carrots in a baking dish. Bring juice to a boil and add the water and cornstarch mixture. Stir and boil for one minute until thick. Pour sauce over carrots in the baking dish.

GOURMET TOMATO SOUP

48 ounces of tomato juice
8 ounces of tomato sauce
½ cup of water
2 tablespoons of sugar
1 bouillon cube
1 tablespoon of chopped celery leaves
½ onion, thinly sliced
½ teaspoon of dried basil
½ teaspoon of whole cloves
1 bay leaf

Combine all ingredients in a lightly greased cooker and stir well. Cover and cook on low for 5 to 8 hours. Remove cloves and bay leaf before serving.

GRANDMA'S MINESTRONE

3 cups of water
1½ pounds of beef, venison or elk
1 onion, diced
4 carrots, sliced
14 ounces of canned tomatoes
10 ounces of frozen, mixed vegetables
1 tablespoon of basil
1 teaspoon of oregano
½ cup of vermicelli, uncooked

Combine all ingredients in the cooker and stir well. Cover and cook on low for 10 to 12 hours.

GREEK CHICKEN

5 potatoes, quartered
3 pounds of chicken parts
2 onions, quartered
1 bulb of garlic, minced
3 teaspoons of oregano
1 tablespoon of olive oil
1 teaspoon of salt
½ teaspoon of pepper

Put potatoes in the bottom of the cooker. Layer with chicken, onions and garlic. Sprinkle seasonings over everything. Drizzle with olive oil. Cover and cook on low for 9 to 10 hours.

HAM BONE SOUP

1 pound of dried navy beans
1 ham bone
6 cups of water

Soak beans overnight in 3 pints of water then drain. Put soaked beans, 6 cups of water and ham bone in a slow cooker, cover and cook on low for 8 hours. Feel free to add favorite spices and vegetables to this basic soup as it simmers.

HAWAIIAN RIBS

3 pounds of spareribs, trimmed
9 ounces of crushed pineapple, canned
½ cup of ketchup
¼ cup of vinegar
3 tablespoons of brown sugar
2 tablespoons of cornstarch
1 tablespoon of soy sauce
½ teaspoon of salt

Combine all the ingredients, except the ribs, in a pan. Stir the mixture and bring to a boil. Cook until thick, stirring frequently. Layer ribs in the slow cooker and pour sauce over the meat. Cook on low for 6 to 8 hours.

HOMEMADE BAKED BEANS

2½ cups of Great Northern beans, dried
4 cups of water
1½ cups of tomato sauce
1 onion, diced
½ cup of brown sugar
2 teaspoons of salt
½ teaspoon of chili powder

Wash and drain beans. Put beans in the cooker with enough water to cover. Put on the lid and cook on low for 8 hours. Stir in remaining ingredients, cover and cook on low for 6 hours.

HUNTER'S CHICKEN

3 pounds of chicken parts
2 cloves of garlic
¼ cup of olive oil
1 small can of stewed tomatoes
1 onion, diced
¼ cup of sweet white wine
2 teaspoons or oregano
1 teaspoon of salt
1 teaspoon of paprika
½ teaspoon of basil
½ teaspoon of rosemary
Pepper to taste

In a pan, brown chicken parts with garlic in the olive oil. Put chicken in the cooker. Mix remaining ingredients together and pour over chicken. Cover and cook on low for 4 to 6 hours.

ITALIAN CHICKEN

1 chicken, in parts
1 can of cream of mushroom soup
1 package of dry Italian salad dressing mix
6 ounces of canned mushrooms, drained
Seasoning salt
Pepper to taste

Put chicken pieces in the cooker. Mix soup, salad dressing, seasoning salt and pepper and pour over meat. Top with mushrooms. Cover and cook on low for 4 to 6 hours.

ITALIAN PORK CHOPS

6 pork chops
16 ounces of tomato sauce
2 cans of green beans, French-cut
½ cup of green pepper, diced
1 onion, diced
1 clove of garlic, chopped
Oil
Water

Brown the pork chops in a skillet with a little oil. Place remaining ingredients in the cooker and stir. Put the pork chops on top of the ingredients. Pour in enough water to cover the chops. Cook on low for 6 to 8 hours.

JERKY CHILI

2½ cups of beef jerky
½ cup of chopped bacon
1 onion, chopped
2 cloves of garlic, minced
2 cups beef broth
4 chili peppers, chopped
2 tablespoons chili powder
2 tablespoons light brown sugar
1½ tablespoons of cumin
5 cups fresh tomatoes, peeled and chopped
½ tablespoon pepper
2 ½ cups kidney or pinto beans, cooked

Cook bacon in deep pot or Dutch oven until fat is released, but not crisp. Add onion and garlic and cook until tender. Add in chili peppers, tomatoes and broth. Cook until tomatoes are soft, 15 to 20 minutes. Now combine chili powder, brown sugar, cumin and pepper and then add to pot. Stir in the beef jerky. Simmer or low boil for 45 minutes. Add beans and boil for about 5 minutes.

KRAUT AND KIELBASA

1 pound of kielbasa, cut to bite-sized chunks
64 ounces of sauerkraut, canned or bagged
1 onion, diced
1 bay leaf

Combine all ingredients in the cooker. Add enough water to just cover ingredients. Cover then cook on high for 30 minutes then cook on low for 6 hours. Remove bay leaf before serving.

LAMB WITH HERBS

6 lamb shanks, cut in half
1 onion, sliced
1 cup of water
2 cloves of garlic, mashed
1 tablespoon of Worcestershire sauce
1 teaspoon of garlic salt
¼ teaspoon of marjoram
¼ teaspoon of thyme
¼ teaspoon of rosemary
¼ teaspoon of fresh ground pepper

Put lamb shanks in a cooker. Mix remaining ingredients together and pour over lamb. Cover and cook on low for 8 to 10 hours.

LAZY CHOPS

4 pork chops
1 can of cream of mushroom soup
¼ cup of ketchup
2 teaspoons of Worcestershire sauce

Place chops in the cooker. Combine remaining ingredients and pour over the meat. Cover and cook on low for 8 to 10 hours.

LOGGING CAMP STEW

2½ pounds of beef, cubed
½ pound of sliced mushrooms
28 ounces of canned tomatoes, crushed
3 cups of beef bouillon
1 cup of celery, diced
4 carrots, sliced
3 potatoes, diced large
3 tablespoons of flour
¼ cup of red wine
1 clove of garlic, crushed
10 ounces of peas, frozen
1 teaspoon of salt
1 teaspoon of pepper
1 teaspoon of Italian herbs
1 teaspoon of Kitchen Bouquet Browning and Seasoning Sauce (optional)

Put everything in a Dutch oven and mix together. Cover and bake at 250 degrees for 5 to 6 hours.

LOW & SLOW CHILI

2 pounds of ground beef, browned & drained
32 ounces of canned red kidney beans, drained
28 ounces of canned tomatoes, diced
2 medium onions, diced
2 cloves of garlic, minced
3 tablespoons of chili powder
1 teaspoon of cumin
1 teaspoon of black pepper
1 teaspoon of salt

Combine all the ingredients in the cooker. Cover and cook on low for 8 to 10 hours.

MEATLOAF

3 pounds of lean ground beef
½ pound of sausage, browned and drained
2 envelopes of dry onion soup mix
1 small can of evaporated milk
1 egg
1 onion, diced
Small potatoes

In a pan, cook and brown sausage in a pan and drain off the grease. Crumble the sausage and mix all of the ingredients into a loaf. Put meat in the cooker and place potatoes around the top. Cover and cook on low for 8 to 10 hours.

MEATLOAF II

2 pounds of lean ground beef
1 onion, diced
2 stalks of celery, diced
1½ cups of cooked rice
1 egg
2 tablespoons of mustard
½ cup of milk

Cook rice, white or wild, according to package directions. Mix all ingredients together and form into a loaf. Place in cooker, cover and cook on low for 8 to 10 hours.

ORCHARD SOUP

¼ cup of raisins
½ cup of dried prunes
½ cup of dried apples
½ cup of mixed, dried fruit
½ cup of Orange Tang
3 ounces or raspberry gelatin
1 cinnamon stick
½ cup of powdered whole milk
1 cup of hot water
Pinch of salt

Put dried fruits in a Dutch oven. Fill with dried fruits and cover with water. Stir in salt, Tang, gelatin and the cinnamon stick. Bring to a boil, cover and reduce to a simmer for 20 minutes or until fruit is tender. Stir dry milk into a cup of hot water until dissolved then add to fruit and thoroughly mix.

OYSTER STEW

20 fresh oysters in juice
1 stick of butter
1 cup of bottled clam juice
1 quart of half & half
¼ teaspoon of paprika
Cayenne pepper to taste
Celery salt to taste
Worcestershire sauce to taste

Put oysters and juice in cooker. Cover and cook on high until their edges curl slightly. Mix remaining ingredients together thoroughly and add to the oysters. Cook on low for 1 to 2 hours.

PEPPER CHICKEN

3 pounds of chicken parts
1 green pepper, diced large
8 ounces of canned water chestnuts, drained and sliced
¼ cup of soy sauce
3 tablespoons of water
2 teaspoons of cornstarch
½ teaspoon of salt

Remove skin and fat from the chicken parts. Put the pieces in the cooker. Combine soy sauce, salt and 1 tablespoon of water and pour it over the chicken. Cover and cook on medium for 90 minutes. Add water chestnuts and green pepper and cook for an additional 30 minutes. Mix cornstarch with 2 tablespoons of water. Stir into the cooker. Cook until thick, stirring constantly.

PIZZA RICE

2 cups of rice, uncooked
3 cups of pizza sauce (thicker the better)
2½ cups of water
6 ounces of canned mushrooms with juice
4 ounces of pepperoni, sliced
1 cup of mozzarella cheese, shredded

Combine all the ingredients except the cheese, in the cooker. Cover and cook on low for 10 hours. Sprinkle with cheese just before serving.

PORK CHOPS & GRAVY

6 thick pork chops, trimmed of fat
2 cloves of garlic, mashed
1 can of cream of mushroom soup
1 can of mushrooms
1 can of tomato paste
Flour
Garlic salt
Salt and pepper to taste
Oil

Season flour with salt and pepper to taste. Dredge chops in the flour mixture. Put a little oil in a pan and brown chops. Put chops in the cooker. Mix together garlic, mushrooms, mushroom soup, and tomato paste with garlic salt, salt and pepper to taste. Pour mixture over chops in the cooker. Cover and cook on low for 8 to 10 hours.

PORK ROAST

3 pounds of pork tenderloin
16 ounces of canned cranberry sauce
1 sliced onion
1/3 cup of French dressing

Slice an onion and lay it on top of the meat. Mix cranberry sauce and dressing and smother the pork with the mixture. Cover and cook on low, about for 8 hours.

POT ROAST

3 pound roast (beef or venison)
2 cups of brewed coffee (not instant)
2 cans of cream of mushroom soup
1 package of dry Lipton Onion soup mix
Flour, salt and pepper

Flour and brown roast in a skillet. Mix remaining ingredients and put in crock-pot with roast. Cover and cook for 8 hours. Recipe works very well on tougher cuts of meat.

REFRIED BEAN DIP

20 ounces of refried beans
1 cup of Cheddar cheese, shredded
½ cup of green onions, diced
¼ teaspoon of salt
Taco sauce to taste

Combine all ingredients in the cooker. Cover and cook on low for 2½ hours. If you're in a hurry, cook on high for 30 minutes, than drop to low for 30 minutes.

RICE PUDDING

2½ cups of cooked rice
1½ cups of evaporated milk
3 eggs, beaten
¾ cup of rice, white or brown
¾ cup of raisin
3 tablespoons of butter
2 teaspoons of vanilla
1 teaspoon of nutmeg

Mix together all ingredients and pour into a lightly greased cooker. Cover and cook on low for 4 to 6 hours. After the first hour stir the pot.

SEAFOOD POT

1 pound of shrimp, peeled and de-veined
1 pound of crabmeat
1 pound of scallops
2 cans of cream of celery soup
2 soup cans of milk
2 tablespoons of melted butter
1 teaspoon of Old Bay seasoning
¼ teaspoon of salt
¼ teaspoon pepper

In the cooker layer shrimp, crab and scallops. Combine soup and milk and pour into the cooker. Mix butter with spices and pour over the top. Cover and cook on low for 3 to 4 hours.

SIMPLE CHICKEN

   4 pounds of chicken pieces
     (works great for wings)
  ½ cup of water
  1 bottle of barbecue sauce (14 to 16 ounces)

Put water in the bottom of the cooker and add the chicken parts. Pour barbecue sauce over the meat. Cover and cook on low for 8 hours

SLOPPY CHICKEN

2 pounds of chicken, diced or shredded
16 ounces of chicken broth
1 can of cream of mushroom soup
1 can of cream of mushroom soup
1 sleeve of butter crackers, crushed

Combine all the ingredients in a cooker and cover. Cook on low for 5 to 6 hours and stir occasionally.

SLOW BURN BEANS

2½ pounds of canned great northern beans, drained
½ cup of catsup
½ cup of brown sugar
½ cup of molasses
1 tablespoon of mustard
1 onion, diced
1 teaspoon of salt
¼ teaspoon of ground ginger
1 pound of bacon, browned and crumbled

Brown bacon in a pan, drain the grease and crumble the strips. Put all ingredients in the cooker, cover and set on low. Cook for 4 hours.

SLOW POKE PORK

3 pounds of boneless pork roast, cubed
2 onions, diced
12 ounces of barbecue sauce
¼ cup of honey

Put meat in the cooker and add onions, honey and barbecue sauce. Cover and cook on low for 6 to 8 hours. When you pull out the meat, you can shred the pork with forks. Serve on rolls, hamburger buns on in a wrap.

SNOW DAY STEW

2 pounds of venison roast in 1-inch chunks
2 tablespoons of olive oil
2 cups of diced onions
2 cloves of garlic
4 cups of acorn squash, diced
1 cup of green onion, diced
1 cup of apple, diced
2 tablespoons of flour
1 teaspoon of cinnamon
1 tablespoon of ground cumin
¾ cup of apple cider
¾ cup of dark beer

In a pan, sauté venison, onions and garlic in the olive oil. Pour these ingredients into a slow cooker or Dutch oven. Cover and cook on low for 5 to 6 hours or until tender.

SOUTH OF THE BORDER BEANS

4 cans of kidney beans
2 onions, diced
2 cloves of garlic, minced
¼ cup of vinegar
2 tablespoons of sugar
1 stick of cinnamon
1 tablespoon of salt
1 tablespoon of dry mustard
3 tablespoons of chili powder
¼ teaspoon of cloves

Place ingredients in the cooker and stir. Cover and cook on low for 8 to 10 hours.

SPICED APPLE CIDER

1 gallon of apple cider
1 cup of orange juice
1 cup of sugar
½ cup of pineapple juice
2 cinnamon sticks
2 teaspoons of whole cloves
2 teaspoons of ground nutmeg
1 teaspoon of cinnamon
1 teaspoon of ground cloves
1 teaspoon of ginger
1 teaspoon of grated lemon zest

Mix all of the ingredients in the cooker, cover and cook on low for 4 to 6 hours. If batch is too large for your pot, halve all of the ingredients.

SPICY PORK CHOPS

6 pork chops
8 ounces of tomato sauce
1 onion, sliced
1 green pepper, sliced in strips
4 tablespoons of brown sugar
2 tablespoons of Worcestershire sauce
3 tablespoons of oil
1 tablespoon of vinegar
1½ teaspoons of salt

Brown pork chops in a pan with the oil then put meat in the cooker. Add remaining ingredients and cover. Cook on low for 6 to 8 hours.

TERIYAKI CHICKEN

3 pounds of skinless chicken pieces
20 ounces of pineapple chunks, canned
1 cup of teriyaki sauce
½ teaspoon of ground ginger

Place chicken in the cooker. Sprinkle ginger over the chicken, pour teriyaki in next and top with pineapple chunks. Cover and cook on low for 6 to 8 hours.

TROPICAL CHICKEN

3 whole chicken breasts cut in half
¼ cup of molasses
2 tablespoons of apple cider vinegar
2 tablespoon of Worcestershire sauce
2 tablespoons of orange juice
2 teaspoons of mustard
¼ teaspoon of hot sauce

Mix all the ingredients into a sauce. Place chicken in the cooker and pour on the sauce slowly. Cover and cook on low for 7 to 9 hours.

TUNA SALAD CASSEROLE

14 ounces of canned tuna
1 can of cream of celery soup
3 eggs, hard-boiled and diced
1 cup of diced celery
½ cup of mayonnaise or Miracle Whip
¼ teaspoon of fresh ground pepper
1½ cups of crushed potato chips

Combine the first 6 ingredients in the cooker. Top with potato chips. Cover the cooker and cook on low for 5 to 8 hours.

TURKEY BREAST BAKE

1 large, boneless turkey breast
¼ cup of apple cider or apple juice
1 teaspoon of salt
½ teaspoon of pepper

Put turkey in the cooker and drizzle with apple cider/juice. Sprinkle salt and pepper on top and bottom of the breast. Cover and cook on high for 3 to 4 hours. When cooking is done, let breast stand for 10 minutes before slicing.

TURKEY CHILI

1 pound of ground turkey
3 pounds of red beans, canned with liquid
1 cup of corn, frozen
1 onion, diced
6 ounces of tomato paste
3 teaspoon of chili powder
3 tablespoons of oil
½ teaspoon of salt

Sauté onion in a pan until it turns transparent. Add turkey and salt and brown lightly. Combine all ingredients in a slow cooker and mix well. Cover and cook on low for 8 to 9 hours.

TURKEY STEW

2 pounds of skinless turkey thighs
15 ounces of tomato sauce
1 pound of carrots, sliced
2 onions, diced
7 potatoes, cubed
4 stalks of celery, diced
3 cloves of garlic, minced
1 teaspoon of salt
2 tablespoons of Worcestershire sauce
2 bay leaves

Place the turkey in the cooker. In a bowl, mix carrots, onions, potatoes, celery, garlic, salt, pepper, Worcestershire sauce, tomato sauce and bay leaves. Pour mixture over the turkey. Cover and cook on low for 8 to 12 hours. Remove bay leaves before serving.

VEGETABLE BEEF SOUP

1 pound of beef, cubed
1 cup of beef bouillon
1½ cups of cabbage, shredded
1½ cups of stewed tomatoes, undrained
1½ cups of corn, frozen or canned
1½ cups of frozen peas
1½ cups of frozen green beans
1½ cups of carrots, sliced
½ teaspoon of salt

Put all ingredients in a cooker. Cover and cook on low for 6 to 8 hours.

VENISON CHILI

2 pounds of ground venison
¼ cup cooking oil
1 cup chopped onion
2 cloves garlic, minced
1 large green pepper, chopped
3 tablespoons chili powder
2 cups tomatoes
1 cup of tomato sauce
1 cup of water
½ teaspoon salt
3 cups cooked kidney beans
1 tablespoon of flour mixed
   with 2 tablespoons of water

Brown venison in oil in a deep pot or Dutch oven until meat loses pink color. Add onion, garlic and green pepper and cook for an additional 5 minutes. Stir in chili powder, tomatoes, tomato sauce, water and salt. Cover and simmer for 2 hours. Add flour paste and cook until mixture thickens. Stir in kidney beans and cook for another 15 minutes.

WHOLE WHEAT & CORNMEAL BREAD

1½ cups of buttermilk
1 cup of whole-wheat flour
1 cup of cornmeal
½ cup of dark molasses
1 teaspoon of baking powder
1 teaspoon of baking soda
½ teaspoon of salt
1 cup of nuts, chopped (optional)
1 cup of raisins (optional)

Make a batter with all of the ingredients. Pour the batter into a greased and floured clean, coffee or similar metal container. Make sure the can that fits loosely in the cooker. The batter should only fill 2/3 of the can. Cover can top tightly with aluminum foil. Put can in the cooker. Pour in enough water into the cooker so that it's filled to ½-inch from the top. Put foil over the cooker and then put the lid on. Cook on high for 4 hours.

WITCHES CAULDRON STEW

1 pound of bacon, chopped and uncooked
1 pound of lean ground beef
30 ounces of kidney beans, canned
28 ounces of canned tomatoes with juice
10 ounces of mushrooms, canned
2 cups of uncooked egg noodles
1 cup of celery, diced
1 cup of onion, diced
2 cloves of garlic, minced
1 teaspoon of pepper
1 teaspoon of seasoned salt
1 teaspoon of cayenne pepper

Brown bacon, hamburger and onion in a Dutch oven and drain the fat. Add celery, onion, tomatoes, beans, noodles and mushrooms plus liquid from the cans. Add seasoning and stir. Bake at 350 degrees for 45 minutes.

WORTH-THE-WAIT BEEF STEW

2 pounds of beef, cut into 1½-inch cubes
6 carrots, sliced
6 small boiling onions, whole
4 stalks of celery, diced
4 cups of boiling water
½ cup of flour
3 tablespoons of shortening
1 onion, sliced
1 clove of garlic
1 teaspoon of salt
1 teaspoon of sugar
1 teaspoon of lemon juice
1 teaspoon of Worcestershire sauce
½ teaspoon of pepper
½ teaspoon of paprika
1/8 teaspoon of cloves

Dredge meat in flour. Melt shortening in the Dutch oven. Add beef slowly and sauté until browned. Keep pieces from touching. Add in all other ingredients except vegetables and stir. Cover and cook over low heat for 2 to 3 hours. Add vegetables and cook for an additional 30 minutes or until vegetables are tender.

Foraged Food

ACORN CAKES

1 cup of acorn meal
1 cup of cornmeal
Water
¼ cup of Honey
1 tablespoon of oil or melted butter
Pinch of salt

Mix the ingredients with enough warm water to make a moist dough but not sticky. Divide the dough into 12 balls. Cover and let the dough rest for 10 minutes or until ready to use. Lightly moisten your hands with water and pat the balls into thick tortillas. Heat an ungreased cast iron skillet on medium high heat. Place the cakes in the skillet. Cook until the edges start to get dry. Lift the cake a little with a spatula to check for doneness. When done, flip over and cook the other side. When both sides are slightly brown they are done.

BEECH LEAVES

2 cups of fresh young beech leaves
¾ cup of boiling water
1 clove of garlic, crushed
1 tablespoon of butter or nut butter
 (wild garlic if possible)

In a pan, combine all of the ingredients and mix thoroughly. Cover and simmer for 8 minutes.

BERRY SOUP

4 cups of Saskatoon or blueberries
4 cups of rhubarb, chopped
4 apples, diced
½ cup of raisins
Water

Clean and wash the fruit and rhubarb. In a pot combine berries, rhubarb, apples and raisins. Cover with enough water to simmer. Bring to a boil then simmer for 30 minutes. Cool and serve.

BIRCH LEAF SALAD

1 cup of young and small birch leaves
1 cup of catkins
¾ head of lettuce, loose leaf (torn small)
6 hard-boiled eggs, diced
1 clove of garlic, minced
½ cup of oil
2½ tablespoons of red wine vinegar
1 tablespoon of mustard
Salt and pepper to taste

Combine leaves, catkins, diced eggs and lettuce and toss. Blend oil, vinegar, mustard, garlic, salt and pepper thoroughly and pour over salad.

BLACKBERRY LEAF TEA

12 blackberry bush leaves
2 cups of water

Bring the water to a boil. Drop the leaves in the water, cover and boil for 5 minutes.

BLUE CAMAS BULBS

½ pound of blue camas bulbs
1 tablespoon of oil, butter or fat
1 tablespoon of lemon juice or
  white wine vinegar
Salt

Remove the papery sheath from the bulbs and place in baking dish with a lid. Pour in just enough water to cover the bottom of the container with a ¼-inch. Cover the container and bake the camas bulbs at 225 degrees for 12 hours. Check after 8 hours or so. You want them to range from pale gold to full gold. Slice the bulbs into rings and lightly dust them with fine salt. Sauté them in oil, butter or fat until they are brown. Keep stirring to prevent them from sticking. When done, toss with lemon juice or white wine vinegar and dust with salt.

BUTTERED NETTLES

2 quarts of young nettle tops
2 tablespoons of sunflower seed oil
1 scallion, diced
½ cup of boiling water
¼ cup + 2 tablespoons of sunflower seed butter

In a pot, sate scallion in the sunflower seed oil for 3 minutes. Add nettles, boiling water and butter. Stir thoroughly then cover and simmer for 20 minutes.

CATTAIL POLLEN CAKES

1½ cups of water
1 cup of sifted cattail pollen
1 cup of fine white cornmeal
3 tablespoons of dried spicebush leaves, chopped
2 tablespoons of sunflower seed oil
1 tablespoon of honey
2 eggs, lightly beaten

Thoroughly mix all ingredients until the batter is smooth. Ladle four cakes of batter onto a hot griddle or hot greased skillet. Cook for 3 to 5 minutes until bubbles form then flip and cook for a few more minutes.

CHAPARRAL TEA

Dried wild lilac leaves
Hot water

Pick and dry these leaves. They leaves are not commercially sold. Steep one teaspoon of dry leaves per cup of hot water. Adjust to taste.

CHICKWEED SALAD

2 pounds of chickweed leaves and steams
½ cup of cider vinegar
4 teaspoons of sunflower butter (or butter)
2 teaspoons of honey
2 teaspoons of sunflower seed oil or vegetable oil

Wash and rinse the chickweed and put it in a large pot. Cover with boiling water and simmer for 3 minutes. Remove from heat and drain the water. Pour cold water over the chickweed to stop the cooking then drain water again. Combine remaining ingredients in the bottom of a large bowl and mix to make a dressing. Add chickweed and toss to coat thoroughly. Chill for 1 to 2 hours.

CHIPPEWA BANNOCK

1 cup of white cornmeal
½ cup of berries
¾ cups of water
5 tablespoons of oil
¼ cup of oil to fry

Blend water, cornmeal, berries and 5 tablespoons of oil thoroughly into a batter. Heat ¼ cup of oil in a skillet and drop spoonfuls of batter into the oil. Flatten the batter into cakes. Cook 4 to 5 minutes per side or until golden brown.

CLAMS & SEAWEED

8 fresh clams with juice
1 quart of water
Seaweed, diced

Dice the clams and reserve the juice. Pour water into a pot and boil. Add clams and juice to the water and seaweed to taste. Reduce heat and simmer for 5 minutes.

CREAMED CHICKWEED

1 fresh bunch of chickweed
Milk
Butter
Salt and pepper

In a pot, parboil the chickweed. Strain the chickweed and chop fine. Mix with a little milk and butter. Salt and pepper to taste and heat.

DANDELION SALAD

4 cups of young tender dandelion greens
4 strips of bacon
3 tablespoons of vinegar
2 teaspoons of sugar
½ teaspoon of salt
¼ teaspoon of dry mustard
Black pepper

Wash and shred the greens. In a skillet fry the bacon until crisp. Remove the bacon and drain on paper towels. Leave the grease in the skillet. In a bowl, place the greens and crumble bacon over it. To the bacon grease and vinegar, sugar, salt, mustard and pepper. Stir the mixture thoroughly and heat. Pour over the greens until wilted and serve.

DRY ROASTED GRASSHOPPERS

1 cup of grasshoppers (dead)
Olive oil
Salt
Pepper
Seasoning of choice (optional)

Spread grasshoppers on a baking sheet and bake at 350 degrees for 10 minutes. Take them out of the oven and toss with olive oil. Sprinkle with salt and pepper to taste. You can also season with garlic salt, onion salt, red pepper flakes or seasoning of choice.

ELDERBERRY TEA

4 cups of fresh, ripe elderberries
2 cups of water

Add berries to the water, mash and stir. Strain the liquid. To make the tea, simmer for a while and sweeten with honey. If it's too strong, dilute to desired flavor.

FIDDLEHEAD STEW

48 fiddleheads
2 cups of boiling water
½ cup of nut butter or butter
1 teaspoon of vegetable or nut oil

Put fiddleheads in a pan and cover with oil and water. Simmer the mixture for 20 minutes or until the fiddleheads are tender. Remove from pan and top with butter or nut butter of choice.

FIREWEED & CLOVER HONEY

10 cups of sugar
2½ cups of water
30 red clover blossoms
30 white clover blossoms
18 fireweed blossoms
1 teaspoon of alum

Wash the blossoms in a colander. In a large pot add water and blossoms and bring to a boil. Remove from heat, cover and lit sit for 10 minutes. Bring to a boil again and add sugar and alum. Boil for 10 minutes. Strain and pour into small, sterilized jars and seal.

FISH AND CATTAILS

2 quarts of cattail shoots or young stems, washed
4 bass or trout fillets
2 cups of water
Salt to taste
Crushed red pepper to taste

Harvest spring cattail shoots or green, new stems. Put fish fillets in a skillet and lay cattails on tops. Pour water into the skillet and cover. Steam for 5 to 10 minutes. Season fish with salt and crushed red pepper.

FRIED MOREL MUSHROOMS

20 fresh-picked morel mushrooms
½ cup of flour
1 stick of flour
1 tablespoon of oil
Salt and pepper to taste

Cut the mushrooms in half. Wash in salted water and remove any bugs or foreign matter hiding in the creases. Drain well. Mix flour, salt and pepper in a Ziploc bag. Drop morels in the bag and shake to coat thoroughly. Heat butter and oil in a skillet slowly. Do not let it burn. Add a few morels at a time, frying 2 to 3 minutes per side.

HAZELNUT SOUP

5 cups of water
2 cups of dried hazelnuts, ground
2 scallions, diced
2 tablespoons of parsley, chopped
1 tablespoon of honey

Put all of the ingredients in a pan, stir and cover. Cook on medium heat for 1 hour. Stir often.

HICKORY MILK

Shelled hickory nuts
Water

Pound the shelled hickory nuts until flat and in pieces. Boil the nuts in water and strain off and save the oily part of the liquid. This is the hickory milk.

HOMESTEADER'S SALAD

2 cups of fresh fireweed shoots
2 tablespoons of wild violet leaves
12 wild violet blossoms
¼ cup of dandelion buds
3 tablespoons of young willow leaves
1 tablespoon of wild chives
Salt to taste
Seasonings or dressing (optional)

Wash all greens in salty water and dry slightly. Put in a sealed bowl or Ziploc bag and chill for at least 2 hours. When serving, salt slightly and sprinkle with seasonings or dressing.

LAMB'S QUARTER GREENS

4 cups of lamb's quarter leaves
Diced scallions
½ cup of water
1 tablespoon of nut butter

Mixed all of the ingredients in a pan, cover and simmer for 5 minutes or until the greens are tender.

LEMON BALM SUN TEA

8 cups of water
16 tablespoons of fresh lemon balm leaves
    (or 8 heaping tablespoons of dried leaves)
1 big jar with a lid
Honey (optional)
Lemon (optional)
Mint (optional)

Pour 8 cups of cool water into the jar and stir in the lemon balm. Leave in the sun for 3 to 6 hours. Strain the tea to remove the leaves. Add honey and lemon or mint to taste.

MAPLE TREE SEEDS
(aka "helicopters")

Maple tree seeds
Butter
Salt
Pepper
Seasoning

After removing the seeds from the helicopter blades, spread them out on a rimmed baking sheet. The green seeds and smaller seeds usually have a better taste. Roast the seeds at 350 degrees for 5 to 10 minutes. If you want to season, sprinkle with butter, salt and pepper or the seasoning of your choice. If you use a dehydrator on the seeds, you can grind them into flour.

MILKWEED SOUP

Top leaves of the milkweed
Blossoms of the milkweed
Salt
Pot of water

Gather the top 4 leaves of the plant in early spring. Pick the little blossoms too. The pot should be half leaves and blossom and half water. Soak the leaves and blossoms for 1 hour in the pot of water. Add a pinch or two of salt. Bring the pot of water to a boil. Boil for 30 to 40 minutes. Stir occasionally.

PINE SYRUP

1 cup of clean pine needles, finely chopped (Spruce or Douglas Fire work best)
½ cup + 2 tablespoons of water
2 tablespoons of corn syrup
Pinch of salt

In a pan mix water, corn syrup and salt. Stir the mixture until boils then let it boil for 1 minute. Remove from heat, add the needles and let it steep for 3 hours. Strain the mixture.

PINON CAKES

3 cups of pinon (pine) nuts
1 cup + 2 tablespoons of water
3 tablespoons of salt
½ teaspoon of salt

Pound the nuts or chop them into a consistency of a course meal. Blend with salt and water and let the batter rest for 1 hour. Heat the oil in a skillet. Form the batter into 8 to 10 3-inch cakes. Brown the cakes on both sides.

RED CLOVER BISCUITS

2 cups of whole wheat flour
½ cup of ground almonds
1 tablespoon of baking powder
¼ cup butter at room temperature
2 eggs, beaten
½ cup plain yogurt
¼ teaspoon vanilla extract
1 cup dried red clover flowers, crushed

In a bowl, mix wheat flour, almonds and baking powder. Stir in butter and knead until a crumbly mixture forms. In a second bowl mix eggs, yogurt and vanilla. Stir in the red clover flowers and blend well. Gradually add cover mixture to the wheat mixture until smooth dough forms. Roll out dough on a lightly floured surface to a thickness of ½-inch. Cut dough in 2½-inch diameter rounds. Use a cookie cutter or a glass. Put the dough rounds on an ungreased baking sheet, Bake at 350 degrees for 15 minutes or until biscuits are golden brown.

RICE, NUTS & BERRIES

2 cups of wild rice
2 wild onions, diced
1 cup of dried hazelnuts, shelled & diced
1 cup of dried blueberries
5 cups of water

In a pot combine rice, onion and water. Bring to a boil then cover and simmer for 40 minutes. Add hazelnuts and blueberries and mix thoroughly. Cover and steam for 20 minutes while stirring occasionally.

SASSAFRASS CHERRY TEA

3 cups of sassafras roots, grated
2 quarts of water
2 cups of wild cherries, crushed
1 cup of honey

Put water, sassafras and wild cherries in a pot. Boil for 10 minutes. Take off the heat and strain the tea. Add honey and drink.

SAUTEED FIDDLEHEADS

20 to 30 fiddleheads, washed and cleaned
5 tablespoons of butter
Salt

Heat butter in a skillet but don't let it burn or smoke. Add the fiddleheads to the butter and sauté in the butter while turning frequently. Cook until they soften. Salt to taste and serve.

SILVERWEED
(Wild Sweet Potato)

Silverweed roots
Water
Seasoning of choice

Gather silverweed roots and put into a pot with water. Boil until they reach the desired consistency. The roots can also be roasted or baked like traditional potatoes. Season with salt, pepper, chives, butter, etc.

SPICEWOOD TEA

Spicewood Twigs
Water
Molasses or honey

Place water and twigs in a pot and boil. Serve the drink hot. Sweeten with molasses or honey. The more twigs you use the stronger the tea.

STEAMED CLAMS

Fresh clams
¼ cup of cornmeal
1 stalk of celery
1 teaspoon of dill seed

Put freshly dug clams in a container with seawater and stir in ¼ cup of cornmeal. Put clams in the refrigerator overnight. Put the clams in a large pot and cover with water. Add in the celery stalk and dill seed. Bring the clams to a boil, cover and remove from heat. Release the steam every few minutes for 20 minutes.

STEAMED MILKWEED PODS

3 quarts of young whole milkweed pods
2 cups of boiling
2 tablespoons of maple syrup
1 scallion, diced

Combine all ingredients in a pan, cover and simmer for 25 minutes while stirring occasionally. Do not let boil.

SUNFLOWER SEED CAKES

3 cups of shelled sunflower seeds
3 cups of water
½ cup of oil
6 tablespoons of cornmeal, ground fine
2 teaspoons of maple syrup

Put water and seeds in a pot. Cover and simmer for 1 hour. Drain the water and grind the seeds into a meal. Mix the seeds meal with cornmeal and syrup. Once stiff dough is formed, shape into 3 or 4 cakes. Pour oil into a skillet and brown the cakes on both sides.

SUNFLOWER SEED SOUP

6 cups of water
2 cups of shelled sunflower seeds
3 scallions, diced
1 tablespoon of dill weed, chopped

Put all ingredients in a pot, cover and simmer for 30 minutes. Stir occasionally while cooking.

WATERCRESS SALAD

1 bunch of watercress, thick stems removed
2 tablespoons of olive oil
1 tablespoon of lemon juice
1 small fennel bulb, thinly sliced
½ cup of pomegranate seeds
Kosher salt
Black pepper

In a large bowl, thoroughly blend olive oil, lemon juice, and a ¼ teaspoon each of salt and pepper. Add watercress, pomegranate seeds and fennel and toss.

WHITE CEDAR TEA

2 large handfuls of white cedar needles
1 teapot full of water
Honey
Lemon juice

Put the needles into the water and boil until the water turns a rich green color. Remove from heat and strain out the needles. Pour a cup of the tea and add a teaspoon of honey and lemon to taste.

WILD GREENS SALAD

2 scallions with tops, diced
1 quart of watercress sprigs
1 quart of wild lettuce leaves
1 cup of fresh mint leaves
½ cup of fresh dill weed, chopped
1 cup of dressing of choice

Toss all ingredients thoroughly and sprinkle with dressing.

WILD LILAC TEA

Dried wild lilac leaves
Hot water

Pick and dry these leaves. They leaves are not commercially sold. Steep one teaspoon of dry leaves per cup of hot water. Adjust to taste.

WILD PEPPERMINT TEA

½ cup of dry peppermint leaves
3-4 cups of water
2-3 tablespoons of honey

Bring water to a boil. Add peppermint leaves and shut off heat. Let tea steep for 5 minutes then pour through a strainer. Add honey and serve.

WILD RICE BAKE

4 cups of wild rice, cooked
¼ cup of soy sauce
1/3 cup of oil
2 teaspoons of onion, diced fine
¼ teaspoon of garlic salt
½ cup of slivered almonds

Combine cooked wild rice with all ingredients and mix well. Pour into a lightly buttered baking dish. Bake at 350 degrees uncovered for 20 to 25 minutes.

WILD STRAWBERRY VINEGAR

1 cup of wild strawberries
1 cup of red wine vinegar

Put the strawberries in a clean jar and crush lightly so the juice is released. Pour in the vinegar and stir thoroughly. Cap the jar and leave in a sunny spot for 4 days. Strain the mixture. Capture the liquid and bottle.

WILLOW BUD SALAD

1½ cups of young, tender willow buds
Oil
Lemon juice
Seasonings of choice

Wash the willow buds and toss with oil, lemon juice or seasonings of choice.

BREAKFAST DAY STARTERS

BAKED OATMEAL

2 cups of dry quick oats
½ cup of sugar
1 egg, beaten
1½ teaspoons of baking powder
½ teaspoon of salt
¾ cup of milk
¼ cup of oil

Pour oil into the cooker to coat the bottom and sides. Add ingredients into the cooker and mix thoroughly. Cover and bake on low for 2½ to 3 hours.

BIG CHEESE OMELET

12 eggs
2 cups of Cheddar cheese, shredded
2 cups of Monterey Jack or mozzarella cheese, shredded
1 cup of milk
Pinch of salt
Tabasco sauce to taste (optional)

Mix together eggs, milk, salt, cheeses and Tabasco sauce. Pour mixture into an ungreased, 8-inch round baking or soufflé dish. Bake at 350 degrees for 55 to 65 minutes.

BLUEBERRY & WILD RICE BREAKFAST

    1 cup of wild rice, cooked
    ½ cup of blueberries
    ½ cup of cream
    2 teaspoons of sugar
    ¼ teaspoon of nutmeg

Pour wild rice and blueberries into a bowl. Sprinkle with sugar and nutmeg. Pour cream over everything.

BREAKFAST BACON PIE

12 slices of bacon, fried and crumbled
1 cup shredded cheese, Swiss or cheddar
¼ cup chopped onion
1 cup Bisquick
¼ teaspoon of pepper
4 eggs
2 cups milk
¼ teaspoon salt

Lightly grease pie plate. Sprinkle bacon, cheese and onion in pie plate. Beat remaining ingredients until smooth. Pour evenly into pie plate. Bake at 400 degrees for 35 minutes. Let stand for 5 minutes before cutting.

BUTTERMILK PANCAKES

2¼ cups of buttermilk
2 cups of sifted flour
2 eggs
2 tablespoons of butter, melted
  (bacon grease is an option)
1 teaspoon of baking soda
1 teaspoon of salt

Sift flour, baking soda and salt together in a bowl. Blend in eggs and buttermilk slowly. Stir until the batter is smooth. Stir in butter. Drop spoonfuls onto a hot, lightly greased griddle or skillet.

FARMER'S BREAKFAST

1 potato, thinly sliced
2 slices of ham, cut into strips
2 eggs, beaten
½ green pepper, cut into strips
¼ tomato, diced
1 onion slice, diced
Oil

In a skillet, fry potato in a little oil until golden brown. Stir in ham, tomato, green pepper and onion. Cook over medium heat for 4 to 7 minutes. Pour beaten eggs over the top. Cook until scrambled to desired consistency. Stir frequently.

FRENCH TOAST

2 cups milk
4 eggs
½ teaspoon salt
2 teaspoons cinnamon
Sliced bread

Beat four eggs thoroughly then mix all ingredients together. Dip bread into mixture until well coated. Fry on an oiled griddle or skillet until golden brown.

FRESH SCRAMBLED EGGS

12 eggs
2 tablespoons of butter
2 tablespoons of whipping cream
¼ teaspoon of salt
Pepper to taste

Combine eggs, salt and pepper and stir briskly. Use a fork or a whisk. Melt butter in a skillet, making sure it coats the bottom. Pour in the egg mixture and stir constantly while cooking over medium-low heat. The eggs should be firm yet moist. Remove from heat and stir in cream.

HAM & EGG SCRAMBLE

1 package of frozen fried potatoes
2 cups cubed ham
1 egg per person
1 small onion
Butter or margarine

Fry potatoes in butter and add diced or chopped onion. Beat eggs and pour over potato mixture. After eggs are pretty well cooked, add ham and cook on low for 15 minutes.

HASH BROWN BREAKFAST

2 pounds of frozen hash browns
1 can of cream of chicken soup
2 cups of sour cream
1½ cups of cornflakes, crushed
1 cup of Cheddar cheese, shredded
1 cup of Monterey Jack cheese, shredded
3 green onions, finely diced
¾ stick of butter, melted

In a large bowl combine soup, onions, sour cream and cheese. Mix thoroughly then add potatoes and mix again. Put mixture into a baking dish. Combine melted butter and cornflakes and sprinkle over the potatoes. Bake at 350 degrees for 1 hour.

MORNING HEALTH SHAKE

2 scoops of low fat yogurt
½ banana
½ cup fresh fruit of choice
1 cup of skim milk
2 ice cubes

Mix all ingredients in a blender, the battery-powered type for those non-electric camps. Or put into a jug and shake until your arms are exhausted.

OMELET IN A BAG

2 eggs
Onion, diced
Cheese, grated
Mushroom, sliced
¼ cup of ham, diced or 4 strips of bacon, cooked and crumbled

Boil water in a large pan. Crack 2 eggs into a quart-sized zip-lock bag. Add onion, cheese, mushroom, bacon or ham in desired amounts. Close the bag and remove excess air. Mix the ingredients by kneading the contents. Place the bag in boiling water for 15 to 18 minutes. Slide the omelet out of the bag and onto a plate.

SEVEN-POUND BREAKFAST

2 pounds of tater tots
2 pounds of sausage or ham in cubes
1 pound of grated cheddar cheese
1 dozen eggs
1 cup of chopped onions
½ cup of milk
Salt and pepper to taste

Butter a 9 by 15-inch baking dish. Put tater tots, meat and cheese in the dish. Thoroughly mix eggs, milk, salt and pepper in a bowl and pour over tots, meat and cheese. Bake at 325 degrees for one hour.

TRAIL BREAKFAST GRANOLA

3 cups of rolled oats
¾ cup of raisins
½ cup of sweetened coconut, shredded
½ cup of almonds, sliced
¼ cup of wheat germ
¼ cup of honey
¼ cup of seeds or nuts of choice (optional)
¼ cup of vegetable oil
2½ tablespoons of water
2 tablespoons of brown sugar
¾ teaspoon of vanilla extract
¼ teaspoon of salt

In bowl 1, mix oats, coconut, almonds, wheat germ and seeds/nuts of choice. In bowl 2, mix honey, oil, water, brown sugar, vanilla and salt. Now pour the wet mixture over the dry mixture and coat thoroughly. Spread the granola mixture on a baking sheet and bake at 350 degrees for 25 minutes. Lightly stir granola every 5 minutes to bake evenly. Mixture is done when it's golden brown. Be careful not to burn.

For more information on the entire series of Tim Murphy's "Cookbooks for Guys" and his other book projects, visit www.flanneljohn.com.

Made in the USA
Columbia, SC
09 December 2018